The Essence of
Personnel Management
and
Industrial Relations

The Essence of Management Series

Published titles

The Essence of Total Quality Management
The Essence of Strategic Management
The Essence of International Money
The Essence of Management Accounting
The Essence of Financial Accounting
The Essence of Marketing Research
The Essence of Information Systems
The Essence of Successful Staff Selection
The Essence of Effective Communication
The Essence of Statistics for Business
The Essence of Business Taxation
The Essence of the Economy
The Essence of Mathematics for Business
The Essence of Organizational Behaviour
The Essence of Small Business
The Essence of Business Economics
The Essence of Operations Management
The Essence of Services Marketing
The Essence of International Business
The Essence of Marketing
The Essence of International Marketing
The Essence of Personnel Management and Industrial Relations
The Essence of Change
The Essence of Managing People

Forthcoming titles

The Essence of Public Relations
The Essence of Financial Management
The Essence of Business Law
The Essence of Women in Management
The Essence of Mergers and Acquisitions
The Essence of Influencing Skills
The Essence of Services Management
The Essence of Industrial Marketing
The Essence of Venture Capital and New Ventures

The Essence of Personnel Management and Industrial Relations

Alan Cowling
Philip James

Middlesex University Business School

Prentice Hall

New York   London   Toronto   Sydney   Tokyo   Singapore

First published 1994 by
Prentice Hall International (UK) Ltd
Campus 400, Maylands Avenue
Hemel Hempstead
Hertfordshire, HP2 7EZ
A division of
Simon & Schuster International Group

Typeset in 10/12 pt Palatino
by Keyset Composition, Colchester

Printed and bound in Great Britain by
BPCC Wheatons Ltd, Exeter

Library of Congress Cataloging-in-Publication Data

Cowling, A. G.
    The essence of personnel management and industrial relations /
Cowling and James.
        p.   cm. – (The Essence of management series)
    Includes bibliographical references and index.
    ISBN 0-13-131848-9 (pbk)
    1. Personnel management.   2. Industrial relations.   I. James.
Philip.   II. Title.   III. Series.
HF5549.C754   1994
658.3–dc20   93-45879
                                                                    CIP

British Library Cataloguing in Publication Data

A catalogue record for this book is available from
the British Library

ISBN 0-13-131848-9

---

1 2 3 4 5   98 97 96 95 94

Contents

v

1
Introduction

We are all affected by personnel management and industrial relations policies and practices. As managers we may be implementing these policies as part of our daily work. If we are senior managers, we will probably have a say in what these policies should be. As employees we are employed under terms and conditions derived from these policies. If we are members of trade unions, we have an influence on these policies through our representatives. And as members of the public we can notice and experience the differences in the quality of service we receive from both public- and private-sector organizations which, in turn, reflect differences in the calibre of staff recruited, the training they have received and the importance they attach to servicing our needs.

This book provides an introduction to personnel management and industrial relations policy and practice for managers and students of management. It is hoped that those on general management and advanced business studies courses, as well as those specializing in personnel management, will find it helpful.

Too often personnel management and industrial relations are treated as two entirely different subjects. Modern practice in organizations is, however, increasingly to bring the two together as part of a policy of creating coherent and effective systems for the management of people. Therefore this book also brings them together. Its other distinctive feature lies in its up-to-date nature and the emphasis placed on presenting the material in a clear and concise fashion without the extended academic passages frequently found in larger texts. References are provided for further reading for those whose appetite for further study has been whetted.

The title of the book has been kept to 'personnel management and industrial relations', notwithstanding the growing currency of the term 'human resource management'. In part this reflects, as the concluding chapter notes, the fact there there is still considerable debate taking place as to what the latter term means. It also, however, reflects the fact that many organizations and academic courses still draw a clear distinction between the two areas of activity.

The book commences with a discussion of manpower planning. The next three chapters then focus on the processes involved in recruiting, motivating and rewarding staff. These are followed by an examination of how employees influence organizational decision-making through collective bargaining and other forms of involvement. The last two substantive chapters then look at the nature, extent and resolution of conflict at work, and the issue of occupational health and safety. The final concluding section provides a brief discussion of the need for organizations to integrate their personnel and industrial relations policies, both with each other and with more general business plans, and considers how far employers are at present achieving such integration.

Readers may choose to read the book from start to finish. However, each chapter has been written to provide a self-contained review of the topic under consideration to aid those who prefer to 'dip' into chapters relevant to their current interests.

2

Planning the organization, planning the people

Organization brings people together for a purpose. As outlined in the previous chapter, organizations today are attempting to clarify their purpose or mission, and to state this in simple terms. Mission statements refer to service quality, satisfying customers, financial return on shareholder capital, maintaining market share or, in the case of public-sector organizations, satisfying political objectives and public needs. In order to achieve their purpose or mission organizations need to be shaped in well-designed structures. Plans then have to be drawn up to ensure that the right numbers and quality of staff are recruited, retained, trained and motivated.

Creating the right kind of organization and ensuring that it is properly staffed requires a considerable amount of planning. Organizations cannot be changed overnight, and it is important to get the structure right. Planning for people also takes time and requires relevant information and well-founded forecasts. The responsibility for this planning is shared between the personnel department, who should be capable of supplying up-to-date information about the staffing situation and forecasts concerning the labour market, line management, who should constantly be thinking ahead about their own departments, and the specialist corporate planning department, who should be looking across the board at markets, finance, operations and human resources. Precisely how the responsibility for planning is shared is a matter that can only be decided by each organization, because there is no magic formula. However, part of the answer lies in the factors examined in the following sections on organization design.

'Structure follows strategy' has been a much quoted maxim of corporate planners in the past. The rule has been that the first priority is to decide on a strategy for markets, products, services and finance. Following this, a structure can be designed to put the desired strategy into place. However, thinking is changing on this order of priorities. Structure is now becoming a primary concern. Asked to state his order of priorities on this issue, Tom Peters, widely regarded as one of the world's leading writers and thinkers on management, recently assigned top weighting to structure, followed by systems and people. Strategy, he argues, should then be set subsequently at strategic business unit level. 'Top management', he adds, 'should be creative of a general business mission'.[1]

Planning the organization

As indicated, the first stage is clarifying the purpose or mission. Subsequently a number of questions have to be answered, in order to decide on the most appropriate type of structure, commencing with the following:

- How centralized or decentralized should we be in our operations and decision-making?
- How many layers do we really need?
- How formal or informal should our manner of operations be?
- Should each member of staff report to only one supervisor?
- What should be the spans of control?
- Should staff be located in departments consisting exclusively of their fellow specialists?

Having attempted to answer these questions, we are in a position to consider the different options available to us.

Designing an organization – the options available

A number of basic models and variations are available. These are:

Model 1: A traditional hierarchical structure

Traditional hierarchical structures are based on theories developed in the first quarter of this century in accordance with so-called 'scientific management' principles. These principles have influenced the design of most medium- to large-scale organization during the first sixty years of the twentieth century.

- Decision-making is located at the top of the organization.
- All staff report to only one superior.
- Spans of control are limited where possible to fewer than ten people.
- Commands and official information must be transmitted through 'proper' channels of information, from the top to the bottom of the organization.
- Staff are grouped by speciality into departments and sections.
- Authority derives from status in the organization's hierarchy.
- Jobs are precisely defined in written job descriptions.
- The so-called line departments are those that directly generate revenue (e.g. sales and production), whereas the so-called 'staff' departments provide a support and advisory service to the line departments (e.g. personnel, accounts).

This model assumes that staff work as individuals and not as groups, and the primary source of motivation is money. Because it treats the organization as a machine, it is given the label of 'mechanistic'.

A special version of model 1 is a so-called 'bureaucratic' structure, widespread in the past amongst public-sector organizations. To the above principles it adds a degree of impersonality whereby staff are selected by a central unit, possess security of tenure and are expected to work strictly within the limits of their job descriptions.

A structure designed on these lines can be represented by a traditional organization chart, shown in Figure 2.1. The possible advantages of this type of structure are stability, conformity and control. The possible disadvantages are inflexibility, inability to change, poor communications and lack of co-operation between departments and the different levels in the organization.

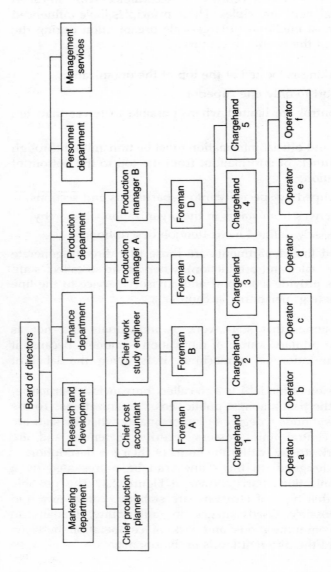

Illustrating: 1. span of control (five or six); 2. line and staff departments;
3. specialization; 4. unity of command; 5. scaler chain; 6. chain of command (six levels).

Figure 2.1 Conventional organization chart (manufacturing concern)

Model 2: An 'organic' structure

An 'organic' structure is in many ways the opposite of a 'mechanistic' structure, and has influenced thinking on the design of organizations for the past thirty years as the limitations of the traditional model were exposed.[2]

- Decision-making is delegated to those with relevant knowledge irrespective of formal status.
- Staff do not have precise job descriptions, and adapt their duties to the needs of the situation.
- Information is informal, and all channels of information are used.
- There is high interaction and collaboration between staff, irrespective of status or department.
- There is an emphasis on flexibility, co-operation, and informality.

Because of its inherent flexibility, it is not possible to capture an organic structure in an organization chart or simple diagram. The possible advantages of this type of organization are flexibility, capacity for change, good communications and concerted team effort. The possible disadvantages are a lack of structure and the inability to mass produce articles requiring repetitive and boring work routines.

Model 3: A matrix structure

A matrix structure is an attempt to overcome the rigidities imposed on organizations by an exclusive allegiance to one department and one 'boss'. Individual members of staff are allocated to a specialist department, representing their 'home' base, but spend most of their time working in mixed teams with staff from other specialist departments on projects, under the day-to-day control of one or more project leaders. There can be further dimensions to a matrix, as when staff also report to a geographically located head office, as in a multinational organization.

A simple matrix 'project' structure is depicted diagrammatically in Figure 2.2. The possible advantages are good team working, good communications and a focus on the tasks to be accomplished. The possible disadvantages are confusion created by different reporting relationships, lack of job security when projects are completed, and

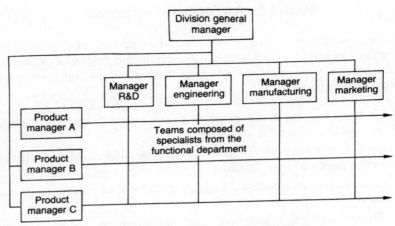

Figure 2.2   A simple matrix project structure

lack of career development as specialization gives way to teamworking.[3]

Variations to basic models

Each model is capable of being varied to some degree by measures including the following:

1. *Divisionalization*. An organization can be split up into divisions. Divisions can be based either on geography, e.g. a 'Midlands' or 'Northern' division, or by product and market, e.g. a 'chemicals' or 'petroleum' division, as portrayed in Figure 2.3. Divisions are co-ordinated from a central headquarters. The possible advantages of divisionalization are that staff are closer to their customers and centralized bureaucracy can be reduced, allowing staff to work better together for a common purpose. The possible disadvantages are loosening of control and a weakening of identification with the present organization.

2. *Decentralization*. Decision-making is delegated as far down the organization as possible. This enables decisions to be made by those with relevant technical expertise, who are closer to customers. One version of decentralization in the private sector is the creation of strategic business units (SBUs) that are smaller than divisions. The possible advantages of decentralization are

the levels of education and professionalism of the workforce are important. A highly qualified professional workforce can, by and large, be left to get on with things; indeed full professionals expect a high degree of autonomy, and prefer to work within a looser organization structure.[9] However, clear objectives and good leadership are still necessary.

5. *Technology of operations.* Technology is changing fast, and a case in point is information technology, which can facilitate decision-making. An example of this is electronic point of sale (EPOS) in stores and supermarkets. Information on precisely what is being purchased is immediately transmitted to warehouses and head office, permitting centralization of purchasing decisions.

6. *Power.* The five factors listed above are rational factors. Power is not a rational factor, but is so important that it must be mentioned. Internal power and politics, with individuals or groups attempting to gain or maintain control of an organization, mean that structures are designed which reinforce the position of the most powerful group or groups.[10] However, should this conflict too much with the rational needs of the organization to survive and change in a dynamic environment, the power élite may lose their jobs.

Planning the people

It is frequently said of the Japanese that their success comes about through careful planning.[11] When the Nissan plant in the north-east of England decided to build the new Micra model, they took on new employees up to nine months before production got under way in order to ensure that adequate training and team development had taken place.[12] This followed very careful selection of new employees.

This process has traditionally been referred to as manpower planning or, more recently, as human resource planning. It aims to provide answers to questions such as:

- How many employees will we need in future?
- What skills will we need?
- What industrial relations will we need?
- What is our current stock of manpower and skills?

- At what rates do we lose staff because of turnover?
- What sort of age structure do we have, and what do we want?
- Should we train our staff, or buy in trained staff?

The penalties for not carrying out manpower planning can be costly. These costs can include not having staff ready and trained to operate new equipment and machinery, having to buy in staff at short notice, hire temporary staff, be faced with the consequences of a spate of unanticipated retirements and, probably most important of all, being unable to deliver a quality service to customers.

The simplest way of tackling manpower planning is by thinking of it in terms of demand and supply. Demand can be forecast from the corporate plans of the enterprise. Supply can be forecast by working out the stock of manpower currently employed, calculating the likely shortfalls and surpluses, and planning accordingly. This process is depicted in Figure 2.5.

Forecasting the likely demand for manpower should be a co-operative exercise between the corporate planners, line managers and the personnel department. Departmental heads should estimate their staffing needs and staffing budgets, a process that normally takes place at least once a year in medium and large organizations. Corporate planners then look across the board at these estimates and propose modifications to take account of forecast changes in markets and technology. At this stage the personnel function can make an input in terms of proposed organization change programmes and on the basis of information held on staffing needs, e.g. from work study programmes.

Demand forecasting can normally be carried out with some degree of precision up to a year ahead – in other words, for as long ahead as markets and services to clients can be accurately forecast. However, longer-term forecasts of two to five years are also needed in order to plan expansion, recruitment, 'downsizing' programmes, and the appropriate training programmes for apprentices and graduates, and multiskilling initiatives. These longer-term forecasts can be revised every year on a 'rolling' basis.

The supply side of manpower planning starts by ensuring that accurate and up-to-date information is available on the current labour force. This means having good personnel records. Organizations employing more than fifty staff should, as a rule, use computerized personnel information systems (CPIS) to facilitate the retrieval and analysis of data.

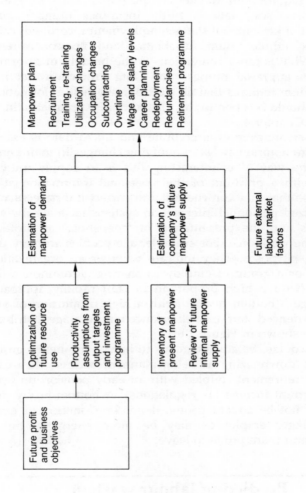

Figure 2.5 Basic manpower planning model, reconciling supply and demand

Personnel records

Data on individual employees should include all the obvious information required for day-to-day purposes, such as grade or status, address, sex, date of birth, insurance number, payroll number, next of kin, marital status, employment record, educational qualifications, ethnic origin, disabilities and fluency in foreign languages. What is more contentious is the holding of information derived from appraisal ratings. The Data Protection Act in the United Kingdom requires that all electronically held information on individuals should be open to their inspection. Appraisal ratings are examined in Chapter 4.

Keeping personnel records accurate and up to date is essential. Employees are notoriously lax in notifying changes in their personal situation. One way of counteracting this is to supply individual employees with a print-out of their personal information at least once a year so that they can check it and correct it if necessary.[13]

Computerized personnel information systems facilitate the analysis of trends and the presentation of 'snapshots' or profiles of sections of the workforce. For example, age profiles are very useful for planning purposes. They indicate whether an organization, a department, or a group of employees sharing a common skill are 'top heavy' (with a high proportion of staff rapidly approaching retirement age), 'bottom heavy' (with a high proportion of young and less experienced staff) or well balanced in their age distribution. Examples are shown in Figure 2.6.

It may, of course, be advantageous to have a top-heavy group of employees if 'down-sizing' is being planned, because they can be offered early retirement coupled with an early pension (in accordance with current income tax regulations). A bottom-heavy profile may or may not be advantageous, depending on current circumstances; younger employees may be more energetic, but less experienced and more prone to leave.

Predicting labour wastage

Labour wastage can be a major drain on staff resources. Steps to improve staff retention are outlined later in this chapter. When planning ahead it is important to take account of likely staff losses

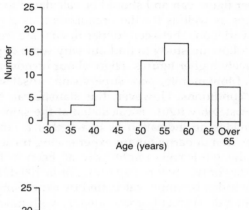

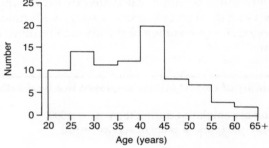

Figure 2.6 Typical age profiles

through wastage, and this means projecting past and present statistics into the future to establish a trend.

Labour wastage can be measured in a number of ways, making use of information from the personnel records database. The most commonly used measure is crude labour turnover on an annual basis. The number of employees who have left in a calendar year is expressed as a percentage of the average number of employees during that year, as shown below:

Labour turnover of clerical officers employed in a local authority

Average number employed during the year = 1000
Number who left employment during the year = 100

Turnover is $\dfrac{100}{1000} \times 100 = 10\%$

This turnover figure can and should be calculated for departments and skill groups as well as for the organization as a whole. Where considerable variations between departments are revealed there needs to be a follow-up study to find out why some departments are showing relatively higher figures. High labour turnover is frequently an indication of low morale, poor supervision, unsatisfying work or poor working conditions. However, this statistic can be misleading unless a labour stability figure is calculated at the same time. This is because it provides no indication as to whether a range of jobs or only a few jobs in a department are experiencing turnover. Thus, in the example, the 100 leavers might have all been in the same job, lasting only a day or two before departing, or in 100 different jobs. A labour stability index is simply calculated by expressing the number of employees in a department or job category with more than twelve months' service as a percentage of the average number employed, as shown below:

Labour stability of clerical officers employed in a local authority

Average number employed during the year = 1000
Number with one or more years of service = 950

Stability is $\dfrac{950}{1000} = 95\%$

Taken together, these two statistics show us that turnover is only a problem in a few of the clerical posts in the example. But for manpower planning purposes we do, of course, need more than one year's figures if we are going to establish a trend and have any confidence in our ability to predict what might happen over the next one to three years. We need data collected over at least a five-year period, such as levels of unemployment, relative pay rates and any other measures of the organization's reputation as an employer.[14]

The likely impact of labour wastage on the stock of manpower over the next few years can be used to predict the numbers likely to remain voluntarily in post. It can also be used as an input into more sophisticated modelling of the flows of manpower between grades. This can be of assistance in deciding promotion rates and in career planning. Mathematical models can be put on a computer program to assist this process. Most models have assumed a traditional hierarchical graded organization structure to predict flows into and out of grades within an organization, as illustrated in Figure 2.7.

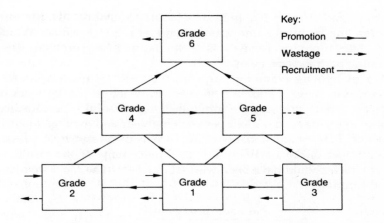

Figure 2.7 Model of manpower flows in a traditional graded structure

In recent years we have experienced a shift away from hierarchical structures with a large number of levels to organizations based on smaller operating units with few layers, described in the first part of this chapter. This trend to simpler structures with very lean staffing levels makes the need for planning even more important, but turns the emphasis on to qualitative changes in the workforce. This requires a prediction of not only how many are likely to remain in employment, but whether they will possess the attitudes and skills that our organization will be demanding. This is one reason why some organizations are placing emphasis on multiskilling and flexibility, enabling employees to tackle a range of tasks and to respond flexibly to as yet unforeseen demands from customers and governments. We will return to this important aspect of contemporary manpower planning in Chapter 5.

Because labour wastage can present so many problems to employers, we cannot leave the topic without examining ways of tackling it and improving retention. In the next two sections of this chapter we examine both labour wastage and absenteeism, which share so many features.

Measuring absenteeism

Personnel management and industrial relations are concerned with achieving a committed and productive labour force; high levels of wastage and absenteeism indicate a failure to achieve this. Manpower planning requires a forecast of attendance, but measures to tackle absenteeism require an analysis of the nature of the problem, so we examine both aspects below.

For manpower planning purposes we need to measure levels of absenteeism over a number of years in order to make a sensible forecast. Three measures of absenteeism are useful – percentage of lost working days, days lost per working year and average length of absence. Percentage of lost working days is calculated by expressing the number of days actually lost as a percentage of the number of days which should have been worked in a year. The most frequently used formula is:

$$\frac{\text{Number of days lost}}{\text{Total number of working days}} \times 100$$

Some organizations prefer simply to state the number of working days lost in a year per category of employee. The third measure is achieved by dividing the number of days lost by the number of absences to calculate the average length of each absence.[15]

An example of the first measure, expressed as a national problem, is provided by a recent Industrial Society survey which showed that the national UK sickness absence rate has recently been running at 3.97 per cent. Absence rates in the public sector were 4.57 per cent, compared with 3.87 per cent in the private sector.[16] The same report estimated that workers in this country take 200 million days sick leave each year, at a total cost of £9 billion. Recent evidence from the Health and Safety Commission claims that sickness costs Britain £25 billion a year.[17] Days lost through sickness varied considerably by industry. On average, transport loses 20 days a year; manual workers in London boroughs, 19.3 days a year; coal miners, 9 days a year; shop workers, 7 days a year; and financial services, 5 days a year; with a national average of 7 days a year. A recent Organization for Economic Co-operation and Development (OECD) report stated that Britain had the worst absenteeism in the industrialized world, losing 113 million working hours each year compared, for example, with France's 51 million.

Measurement reveals the size of the problem. Yet it is a problem that many organizations do not take seriously, to their cost. It may be that because most of absenteeism is put down to sickness there is a feeling that little can be done. However, this is not the case. Some organizations achieve far better absenteeism levels than others. How is this done?

Controlling absenteeism and wastage

Absenteeism and labour wastage represent a decision by the employee not to turn up for work. Therefore, if we can find out why employees are not turning up for work or are quitting their jobs, we shall be in a position to rectify the situation.

Of course, some non-attendance is not voluntary. Employees may be too ill to come to work or may have suffered a major domestic crisis. Therefore, we must assume that there is a basic minimum level below which it is unreasonable to expect non-attendance to fall. As we have noted, the national average for sickness-related absenteeism is 7 days a year. Some organizations achieve considerably lower figures. Research and common sense both point to a number of factors that influence non-attendance. These include the penalties for non-attendance, the expectation that non-attendance is being closely monitored, the commitment of employees to the work they are doing, the degree of job satisfaction achieved at work and relationships with fellow workers and supervisors. A comprehensive list of these factors is provided in a model devised by Steers and Rhodes (Figure 2.8).[18] This model provides a comprehensive checklist for employers, who can conduct their own investigation to see whether their absenteeism and wastage are primarily caused by one of the seven factors illustrated, or by a combination.

If measurement indicates that there is a problem, the first stage is to locate where it exists, i.e. in which departments, or categories of employee. The second stage is to try to find out the cause or causes of the problem by interviews with staff and supervisors and the use of questionnaires. Steps to tackle the problem can then be initiated, and followed up to see if they are working. An example of a successful scheme is provided by Figure 2.9, which had the desired effect of reducing absenteeism to a satisfactory level.

Controlling labour wastage requires a similar approach, namely measurement, location of the problem, finding the reasons, implementing measures and reviewing progress. The most significant difference, however, lies in the difficulties in establishing why people are leaving. When people give in their notice it is important that they should be interviewed by their head of department and, in some cases, by a personnel executive. They may also be asked to state their reason for leaving in writing or by ticking the reason on a short list of possible reasons. However, the fact is that leavers are frequently reluctant to tell the truth, the whole truth and nothing

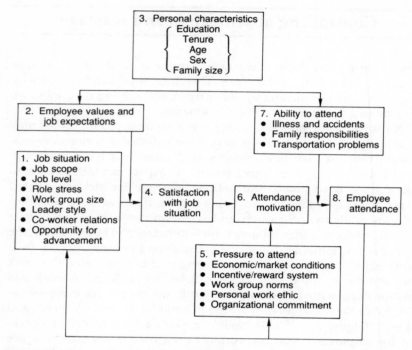

Source: Steers, R. M. and Rhodes, S. R., 'Major influences on employee attendance: a process model', *Journal of Applied Psychology*, August 1978, p. 393.

Figure 2.8 Explaining and predicting absenteeism and wastage

but the truth about their reasons for leaving. They may not wish to upset people, or may be afraid to tell the truth, or not wish to jeopardize the reference they may need from their employer. Following up staff after they have left usually results in a very poor response. There is no easy solution to this problem, although a trained interviewer can usually get somewhere near the truth.

A more positive way of tackling labour wastage is to focus on why people stay, rather than why they leave. As the overriding objective is to achieve high levels of productivity and motivation, it is important to find out why staff stay, and what they find good about the job, as well as their criticisms. This enables management to deal not only with complaints but, more importantly, to enhance the positive aspects of their employment package. To do this properly requires an attitude survey, a topic examined in Chapter 5.

RANK XEROX
Welwyn Garden City

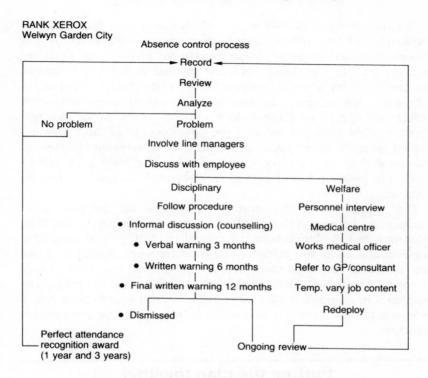

Figure 2.9   Example of an absence control process

Adding a strategic dimension

At the outset of this chapter we emphasized that manpower planning takes its lead from corporate mission, and in turn aims to support corporate plans. Within the past decade it has been realized that the way human resources are planned, organized and motivated is a strategic issue, going beyond manpower plans which simply aim to achieve a balance between supply and demand forecasts. This important point was made in the introductory chapter to this book. The term 'strategic' is much misused these days, but used properly it describes the achievement of long-term corporate goals and, in the last resort, the survival of the organization. A good illustration of strategy is provided by the ICL case study presented at the end of this chapter.

Commenting on another major British enterprise, Paul Evans at INSEAD business school says 'The corporate board of ICI has essentially two tasks today: major investment and strategic decision-making on the one hand, and the management of key human resources on the other'. Strategic issues that relate to people are currently seen in major organizations as organization structures, culture change, management development, performance management, reward management and the development of flexible multi-skilled teams.[19] These topics are dealt with in relevant chapters of this book, but are listed here to emphasize that they must not be tackled in isolation but as part of an integrated approach to human resources.

The implication of this strategic dimension for the process of manpower planning is that key features may be selected by the chief executive and executive board as crucial to strategy and long-term survival and given top priority. The most frequent examples of this are decisions to implement major reorganizations and culture change programmes. These initiatives have the effect of shifting the emphasis in manpower plans in a radical way towards achieving a new equilibrium between demand and supply in the reorganized structure.

Putting the plan together

An examination of the supply forecasts in the light of the demand forecasts will indicate the areas where special initiatives are required to achieve balance. It is normal to draw up plans for action under a conventional list of functional headings, for example:

- Recruitment and selection. In which key areas should recruitment take place over the next twelve months?
- Training. What are the training and development priorities, and how should they be phased?
- Redundancies. Where are redundancies likely to occur, and how should we set about consulting interested parties and arranging out-placement or retraining activities?
- Industrial relations. How should we maintain good relations with various worker representative groups and improve consultation and communication?
- Motivation. What new reward management initiatives and other measures to improve motivation are called for?

- Productivity and flexibility. What measures to improve productivity and flexibility, such as teamworking, are called for?
- Performance management. How can performance be managed better? Do appraisal schemes require review?
- Management development. What management development programmes are needed to develop appropriate competencies in managers in pursuit of new performance targets?

Clearly there is overlap between these areas, but that is the way it should be. Manpower plans must be integrated into a concerted drive by line managers and personnel managers to achieve organizational goals.

A human resource planning case study – ICL

This case study provides a good illustration of how a leading company has integrated planning for organization and people into its business policy.

The context

ICL started in 1968 as a conglomerate of small UK computer firms drawn together by government pressure. It flourished in the 1970s, taking over Singer Business Machines in 1976, but ran into difficulties in the 1981 recession. Again, the government came to the rescue, supporting a rescue package. Two outstanding managers were recruited from Texas Instruments, Robb Wilmott and Peter Bonfield. In 1984 it was taken over by STC, and Bonfield took over as managing director. He cut unprofitable divisions, introduced new staff training programmes and merit-related pay, delegated responsibility and placed great emphasis on quality. In 1990 ICL was in a much healthier state than its European rivals, making £100 million profit on a turnover of £1.6 billion, employing 21 000 people and operating in seventy countries with 40 per cent of its turnover based on overseas business. Then in 1991 it was sold by STC to Fujitsu of Japan. This gave ICL the backing of the second largest information technology company in the world, and Fujitsu a foothold in Europe. ICL in turn then purchased Nokia Data, the Finnish computer group, to increase its European presence.

Mission and strategy

The company states 'ICL is an International Company dedicated to provide profitable high value customers solutions, for improved operational and management effectiveness'. Its key strategies are:

1. High value systems to defined markets.
2. Commitment to open systems – providing customers greater flexibility in choice of manufacturer.
3. Collaborations – to gain market or technical leverage.
4. Organizational responsiveness – to react to the fast-changing market.
5. Focus on systems and solutions for the customer.

Culture and mission

In 1982 ICL published a statement on its values and beliefs entitled 'The ICL way', which was distributed to all staff. It contained the following seven commitments:

1. Commitment to change: 'Adapt to succeed'.
2. Customers: 'The customer matters most'.
3. Excellence: 'Can do – or can't progress'.
4. Teamwork: 'One plus one equals three'.
5. Achievement: 'Results win rewards'.
6. People development: 'Real development is self-development'.
7. Productivity showcase: 'Show the world'.

In order to obtain the culture change required to achieve this mission statement, ICL focused on three elements seen as essential to success: top management vision and determination, education and communication and supporting processes and systems (Figure 2.10).

To quote Don Beattie, their personnel director, 'we have to have all three to be successful'. Ten years after publishing their mission statement ICL have been more successful than the majority of large organizations in this country in moving to a new culture and in achieving business objectives in a highly competitive market.

Linking manpower plans and business plans

Like many similar organizations, ICL conducts an annual business planning cycle. This commences at the end of the calendar year. A framework is prepared for the five-year strategic plan, developed by line units in the period January to March, and reviewed centrally in April. These reviews of the strategic plans form the basis for the operating plan guidelines for the next company year, which are issued in May/June, and form the basis for budget guidelines. The whole process is shown in Figure 2.11. However, what is important in this context is the way manpower plans are integrated into this process via what is termed the Organization and Management Review (OMR) in April, which considers the organizational implications of the five-year strategic plan. Organiza-

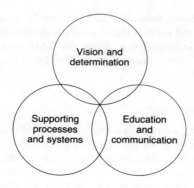

Figure 2.10   Three elements of culture change at ICL

Date	Activity	QBR focus*	OMR focus†
Nov. Dec.	5 year strategic plan guidelines		
Jan. Feb.		End of year actual	Individual development
April	5 year strategic plan complete	Strategic plan	Organization strategy
June	Budget guidelines		
July Aug.		Mid-year review	Organization SWOT and initial view of plan to delivery of budget
Sept.	Budget reviews		
Oct.		Forecast/ budget	Organization for budget year

*Quarterly Budget Review.
†Organization and Management Review.

Figure 2.11   Organization and management review process at ICL

tion and Management Review meetings are conducted between the managing director and each of the executives that report to him, with the personnel director in attendance. Thus the OMR process is 'owned' by line management. This process then drives subsequent manpower planning.

Manpower planning outcomes

Detailed manpower planning is subsequently undertaken at each of the main subunits reporting to the managing director. Using a company-wide categorization of skills, the units are able to look forward from two to five years to assess the skill shifts required to support the business plan. At the centre the company also reviews the requirements for new skills and productivity indexes between similar line units across the company.

Areas of human resource management which have been featured in recent ICL manpower programmes include the following:

- Culture change. As well as publicizing the mission statement, ICL has implemented a cultural training programme based on 'Quality as a way of life'.
- Performance management. This incorporates appraisal, objective setting and reward systems.
- Management development at four levels, for strategic managers, business managers, first line managers and new managers.
- Training at unit level to develop multiskilled workers and flexible work teams.

Source acknowledgements

Beattie, D. F. and Tampoe, E. M. K., 'Human resource planning for ICL', *Long Range Planning*, **23**(1), 1990, pp. 17–28.
Caulkin, S., 'ICL's Lazarus act', *Management Today*, January 1987.
Lorenz, A. and Robinson, P., 'Japanese force IBM revolution', *Sunday Times*, 1 December 1991.
Steel, S., 'Profile on Peter Bonfield', *Management Today*, January 1992.

References

1. Peters, T., *Liberation Management*, London: Macmillan, 1992, p. 13.
2. Burns, R. and Stalker, G. M., *The Management of Innovation*, London: Tavistock, 1961.
3. Davis, S. M. and Lawrence, P. R., 'The problems of matrix organisations', *Harvard Business Review*, May–June 1978.

4. Allen, S. A., 'Organisational choices and general management influences networks in divisionalised companies', *Academy of Management Journal*, September 1978.
5. Lawrence, P. R. and Lorsch, J. W., *Organisation and Environment*, Boston, MA: Harvard University Press, 1967.
6. Peters, *Liberation Management*.
7. Pugh, D. S., Hickson, D. J., Hinings, C. R. and Turner, C., 'The context of organisational structure', *Administrative Science Quarterly*, 14, 1969, pp. 378–98.
8. Kanter, R. M., *The Change Masters: Corporate entrepreneurs at work*, London: Allen and Unwin, 1982.
9. Lorsch, J. W. and Matthias, P. E., 'When professionals have to manage', *Harvard Business Review*, July–August 1987, pp. 78–83.
10. Hinings, C. R., Hickson, D. T., Pennings, J. M. and Schneck, R. E., 'Structural conditions of intraorganisational power', *Administrative Science Quarterly*, March 1974, pp. 22–4.
11. Ohmae, K., *'The Mind of the Strategist – The art of Japanese business'*, New York: McGraw-Hill, 1982.
12. *Annual Report, 1991*, Nissan Motor Manufacturing (UK) Ltd.
13. Carolin, B. and Evans, A., 'Computers as a strategic personnel tool', *Personnel Management*, July 1988.
14. Bevan, S., *The Management of Labour Turnover*, IMS Report No. 137, Institute of Manpower Studies, June 1987.
15. IDS Study, *Controlling Absence*, Study 498, Incomes Data Services, January 1992.
16. Industrial Society, 'Survey of absenteeism in the UK – Industrial Society survey', *The Times*, 11 March 1993.
17. Thomson, A., 'Unhealthy trends in Britain's sick leave', *The Times*, 12 June 1991.
18. Steers, R. M. and Rhodes, S. R., 'Major influences on employee attendance: a process model', *Journal of Applied Psychology*, August 1978.
19. Johnson, G., 'Managing strategic change – strategy, culture and action, *Long Range Planning*, 15(1), 1992, pp. 28–36.

3

Recruitment and selection

Because organizations consist of people, and because it is people who achieve success or failure, the success of an organization is determined sooner or later by the calibre of its recruits and by the effectiveness of its recruitment and selection policies. Careful attention to recruitment and selection pays dividends, a fact well known to our leading companies as well as to Japanese companies setting up in Britain.

It is customary to distinguish between recruitment and selection, and to pay more attention to selection. However, such emphasis is not managerially sound. Selection is the final stage in the recruitment process, and there is little point in utilizing the best selection techniques in the world if the earlier stages of recruitment are not well managed and less than satisfactory candidates are being attracted to apply for vacancies. It is equally important to minimize the need for recruitment and selection by a positive policy on manpower retention and controlling labour turnover. As indicated in the previous chapter, labour turnover is expensive, and most recruitment is carried out in order to replace losses. Prevention is better than cure.

Some losses will of course occur, and new positions will be created which need to be filled. All organizations require an infusion of new blood from time to time. Taking its cue from corporate strategy and manpower plans, a recruitment policy that has the full support of top management needs to be in place and constantly monitored.

Recruitment policy

The aim of recruitment policy should be to attract good-quality applicants and to make valid, reliable and cost-effective selection decisions. Recruitment policy begins by considering the best ways in which to attract good-quality applicants.

Whether good-quality applicants apply for vacant positions depends on a number of factors, of which the following are probably the most basic:

- Has the vacancy been drawn to or attracted their attention?
- Do the salary and conditions of service look attractive?
- Can they do the job?
- Does the job itself look interesting and satisfying?
- Does the company have a good reputation as an employer?

If we take the last point first, we need to consider how an organization gains a reputation as a good employer. Large UK organizations such as Marks and Spencer, ICI, British Gas and the National Health Service enjoy differing reputations as employers. Small firms, likewise, enjoy differing reputations in their local labour markets. While it may take a good few years to build up a reputation as a good employer, this reputation can unfortunately be lost in months, or even weeks, by injudicious employment decisions, such as the well-publicized sacking of a group of employees in a harsh and unsupportive manner.

The head of external liaison for British Airways was recently quoted as saying that potential employees are as likely to be influenced by the overall image of a company as by the salary mentioned in an advertisement.[1] In a reported survey of 1000 employees, staff were asked to identify the five most important things they looked for in a job. Sixty-six per cent said having an interesting and enjoyable job, 52 per cent said job security, 41 per cent said feeling they had accomplished something worth while and 37 per cent said basic pay. Other staff surveys have obtained similar results.[2]

Because of these considerations, organizations must review their recruitment policies at regular intervals to check that they are actually offering the conditions and job opportunities that good applicants are looking for. In the next chapter we go on to examine ways of checking on whether pay and conditions of service are competitive.

The labour market

Manpower plans and recruitment plans must take account of the labour market, both at local and national levels. At local levels, this means being well informed about the supply and demand for recruits within an area defined by daily travel to work patterns. Many manual workers are reluctant to work more than five miles away from where they live. Office workers will travel considerably further if public transport is good. Within this local labour market area there may be other employers expanding or contracting their demand for manpower. There will be local schools and colleges sending young people into the labour market. New housing estates may be being built. At a national level trends such as demographic change and changes in the output of college leavers may be significant for recruitment planning. Some organizations rely on a large intake of school-leavers every summer. Engineering companies may depend on an intake of new engineering graduates every autumn. From time to time various skill shortages affect the national labour market, especially during economic upturn, causing employers to complain bitterly. Some of these skill shortages are a direct result of employers cutting back on their training programmes in previous years.

Demographic change is the easiest national trend to anticipate because it is so well documented. Yet employers are still caught out and surprised. The current decline in the number of school-leavers was caused by the drop in birth rates fifteen to twenty years ago. As this decline has coincided with economic recession it has not had as much impact as was anticipated, although the consequences are still to be experienced fully. Figures 3.1 and 3.2 illustrate two important dimensions of recent demographic change. While fewer young people are entering the labour market, more women are seeking employment, particularly on a part-time basis.

If shortages are anticipated, companies have a variety of options to consider. Putting up rates of pay is only one option, and may be self-defeating as other employers follow suit. Other options include the following:

- better training;

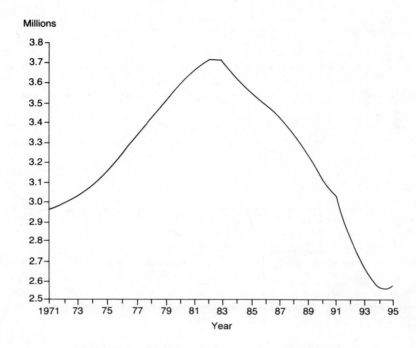

Figure 3.1   Population aged 16–19, Great Britain

- better retention of staff;
- better relations with local schools and colleges;
- more flexible use of labour;
- a more positive attitude to minority ethnic groups;
- the employment of older workers.

Employment costs and the recruitment process

Employing people costs money. Making a decision to employ someone is equivalent to making an investment decision costing thousands of pounds. Here are some considerations.

In addition to basic salary, indirect benefits such as insurance, holidays and pensions add another 30 per cent to employment costs.

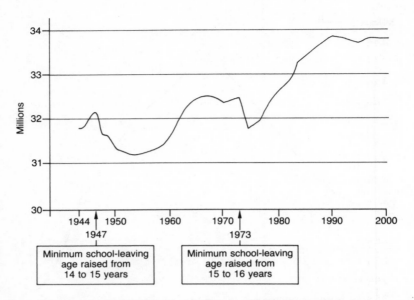

Figure 3.2 Population of working age, 1944–2000, Great Britain

Then there is the cost of providing office or factory space, equipment and machinery. Add to this the cost of recruiting, selecting
and training each new employee, and the costs mount up again. A
basic salary of £15 000 may become a cost of £20 000 a year, plus a
further £5000 in equipment and support services. Initial recruitment
and selection costs can easily add at least another £1000 per head.
Because employees can no longer be hired and fired at whim, and
are protected by employment legislation, employment costs should
be treated as quasi-fixed costs in accounting terms, rather than
variable costs.

Another way of thinking about costs is to consider the cost of a
bad selection decision. One bad apple can soon upset the rest. A
bad employee can upset colleagues, customers, supervisors and
subordinates. The result is further cost. Good selection pays, poor
selection costs.

All of this adds up to the need to give careful consideration before
proceeding with employment. Is it essential to fill the vacancy? Can
the work be redistributed? Have we a suitable internal candidate?
Does our manpower plan support recruitment at this time? A
sensible sequence for tackling recruitment and selection that takes
account of these important questions is provided in Figure 3.3.

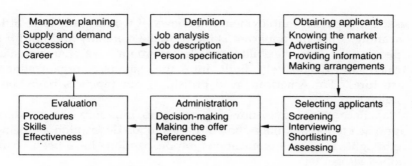

Figure 3.3 Optimal sequence for recruitment and selection

Job definition

Good recruitment and selection requires accurate definition of what we are looking for. This in turn depends on accurate and up-to-date information on the job to be filled, and likely future developments in the job and demands on the job holder. Traditionally, the basis for job definition has been provided by job analysis and job description. Job analysis is the process of analyzing a job to find out the true contents of a job, and was originally devised by work-study specialists and, later, borrowed by personnel specialists. The findings of a job analysis are recorded in a job description, which should provide a clear outline of a job, its tasks, responsibilities and conditions.

Job descriptions have traditionally provided information for the job definition, and have therefore formed the basis for recruitment and selection. Job descriptions have also provided the basis for rates of pay, training programmes and staffing establishments. Indeed, job descriptions have traditionally been seen as providing the basis for most personnel practices. But this is now changing.

It has come as a shock to many Western managers to find that successful Japanese companies do not use detailed job descriptions. Japanese employment philosophy is radically different. A well-known American authority on Japan, Arthur Whitehill, puts it succinctly 'a fundamental principle in American management is to start with a job. Job analysis, job description, job specifications, and job evaluation are almost sacred procedures in American companies. After all, most personnel procedures rest firmly on this foundation. Seldom if ever would the question ("what does the job pay?") be asked in Japanese employment interviews. It would really have little meaning, since the applicant is hired by the company and not for a specific job. Thus flexibility and "elbow-room" are characteristics which are deliberately built into the Japanese organizational structure.'[3] For American, read British, as our practices have been similar.

Japanese thinking is now beginning to influence the Western approach to job definition, and attitudes to job description are being rethought. In some organizations job descriptions have been abandoned altogether.

Job specifications

Similar changes are taking place in relation to job specifications. 'Job specification' is a widely used term that describes the process of transforming the job description into a definition of the kind of person who might successfully carry out the job. As well as Japanese influences, job specifications are now being affected by new thinking on the importance of 'key result' areas, in addition to interest in the concepts of competence, competency and competencies.

For many years job specifications in Britain have been drawn up using a framework of headings derived from work by the occupational psychologist Alex Rodger. He named his framework 'The Seven Point Plan', advising that use of the following seven headings would enable organizations to match job applicants and jobs: physique, attainments, general intelligence, special aptitudes, interests, disposition, and special circumstances. A more modern framework for drawing up a job specification advocates the use of six factors:[4]

1. Physical attributes. The physical requirements of the job.
2. Mental attributes. The intellectual demands of the job.
3. Education and qualifications required for the job.
4. Experience, training and skills needed.
5. Personality. Personal qualities required in the job.
6. Special circumstances. Points not covered by the first five factors.

Drawing up a job specification prior to recruitment is still an important stage to go through in order to build up a clear picture of the person needed to fill the job. It is also useful to specify not only what are the desirable qualities, but also what are the essential qualifications being looked for, thus providing a 'bottom line' below which one must not drop when carrying out selection.

Examples

Clerical supervisor in a large office

Factor – education and qualifications
(a) *Desirable*. Higher National Diploma in business studies.
(b) *Essential*. National Diploma in business studies, or 'A' level in business studies plus GCSE grades in English and mathematics of grade C or above.

In addition to preparing a job specification, time should also be spent on clarifying what are the key result areas for the job in question, in the manner described below.

Key result areas

Key result areas (KRAs) are a statement of the most important results expected from a job holder. KRAs are important because they:

- provide goals for the job holder;
- indicate what the job is really about – getting results;
- put the emphasis on outputs and not on inputs;
- clarify for new recruits what is expected of them;
- provide a basis for appraisal and performance management.

What are key results?

- They are outcomes and outputs, not tasks or actions.
- They describe success criteria which are explicit and unambiguous.
- They are stated in terms of quality, quantity, cost and time.

Example

Key result area: Achieve more effective management appraisal

Specific results:

1. To develop and run workshops on appraisal for 30 per cent of managers by November at a cost of £20 000.
2. Issue performance questionnaires and notes to all appraisers by July of this year.
3. To resolve queries within two working days.

Language used in job specifications and key result area statements

As already indicated, for too long job descriptions have been seen as dull and lifeless descriptions of the contents of a job. As pressures mount on organizations to be more competitive and to provide better-quality service, the culture has to be changed to one of stimulating employees to a more active participation in achieving organizational goals. This culture can be encouraged by using language that supports output and change. This applies particularly to the use of verbs. Good examples are verbs such as achieve, attain, change, complete, create, establish, generate, grow, improve, initiate, launch, motivate, reduce, reorganize and update.

Competencies and selection

Job specifications can also be strengthened by using a modern competency-based approach. Competency has been defined as 'an underlying characteristic of an individual which is causally related to effective or superior performance on the job'. Competencies can encompass motives, traits, self-concepts, knowledge and cognitive and behavioural skills, and are considered again in the next chapter in the context of performance management. The point to note here is that developing a relevant list of competencies and distinguishing between satisfactory, good and excellent levels of achievement do require a thorough internal investigation in order to establish the types of behaviour distinguishing good performers from moderate performers. These types of behaviour can then be written into the job specification to help us select high performers.[5]

An example of a list of competencies relevant to selection and appraisal for a senior position requiring both professional and managerial competencies might cover; planning and project management, communication, teamworking, problem-solving, customer focus, leadership, delegation, managing change and performance management. Behaviour leading to good performance under each of these headings can then be researched within the organization by a careful observation of successful and not so successful managers.

Finding applicants

'Finding applicants' may seem a strange title at a time when thousands are seeking employment. But in almost all cases what is required is a sufficiency of good candidates – no more and no less. The existence of too many applicants, especially if they are not suitable, creates embarrassment, is time consuming, and costly. Too few applicants, and the choice becomes too limited. Ideally, a short list of well-qualified candidates is required from which a final selection can be made. How is this best achieved?

The first decision is whether to conduct the search oneself, or to make use of external agencies and consultants. This will depend on a number of factors, including the competence and resources of the personnel department, the seniority of the position, and the anticipated difficulties in finding suitable applicants. Where the job is relatively straightforward and applicants are likely to be in good supply, the vacancy can normally be handled internally. It is also a good idea to advertise vacancies internally, in order to encourage staff to develop their careers. A good computerized personnel records system helps to identify current employees suitable for vacancies.

For straightforward office vacancies it is frequently advantageous to use agencies, who should have a list of suitable candidates, although they will charge a fee proportionate to the first year's salary figure. When searching for someone to fill a senior position, or a specialist in short supply, the services of consultants or executive search agencies may be advisable. The fees will be high, amounting to thousands of pounds in the case of senior staff, but the costs have to be weighed against the benefits. When using external consultants it is most important to have a clear idea of what one is looking for; consultants should be servants and not masters. A carefully prepared job specification is therefore essential.

Advertising for staff

There are many sources of potential recruits, ranging from responders to factory-gate notices, relatives and friends of existing employees, and government Job Centres, to advertisements in the media. Some are free, such as Job Centres, some are expensive. Over a period of time the personnel department should keep a record of the cost and the effectiveness of these different sources of applicants, to determine which offer the best value for money.

Advertising for staff in the press is big business. Nearly £470 million was spent by employers and their agencies in 1987, before the onset of the recent economic recession.[6] As a result, a sophisticated and thriving business has grown up. If use is going to be made of advertising agencies, considerable care has to be taken in their selection. The professional body for UK advertising agencies is the Institute of Practitioners in Advertising (IPA), who operate a register of members. If a large-scale advertising campaign is planned, selected agencies can be asked to make presentations to the company, and the most convincing one can then be appointed. If occasional press advertisements are planned, then it is a good idea to appoint an agent to advise on the advertisement, to set it in copy form, and to place it in the desired newspapers or journals. Agencies book space in advance in the press, and it is frequently impossible to place an advertisement at short notice unless one goes through an agent. Agencies take a commission from the press, and therefore can frequently offer good-value service to employers.

What should a good advertisement include by way of information? More importantly, what do potential recruits want to see in advertisements? Evidence from surveys indicates that the priority items are as follows:

- place of work;
- salary;
- closing date for applications;
- how to apply;
- relevant experience;

- qualifications;
- duties;
- responsibilities;
- the organization.

It should be remembered that advertising for staff is a form of selling – selling the job and selling the company in order to achieve the desired response. It is therefore a good idea to start by asking the question: why should somebody want to do this job? Selling points should then be listed. A typical list might be: job interest, training provided, remuneration, technology, location. Following this, decisions can be made on the main headline, subheadings and copy. Make sure that the instructions on how to apply are clear. Today styles of advertising tend to be colloquial. Avoid pomposity and keep language simple and factual. Ensure synergy with the overall corporate advertising style. Monitor the results.

Short listing

For most vacancies the objective of a recruitment campaign is to create a short list of suitable candidates who match the requirements of the job specification. Provided a list of essential and desirable requirements has been listed in the manner recommended earlier, then, in theory at least, it is a simple matching process, matching the applicant's profile against that required by the job. However, if large numbers apply, this can be time consuming. It also requires a well-designed application form.

Application forms should be designed to aid the selection process. They should also be designed with an eye to the organization's personnel information system, because personal data on the application form can be used for record purposes should the applicant be appointed and commence work. For selection purposes the application form should incorporate the framework currently being adopted for job specification purposes. Factors such as education, qualifications, work experience, training and special skills feature on most application forms, plus space for statements on health and disabilities. However, personality remains a contentious area. Space is normally provided for a description of leisure interests, as this may provide some indication of personal characteristics, especially with school and college leavers (we will return to the subject of personality in the context of psychometric testing). It is also useful to leave free space for candidates to indicate why they think they are suitable for the position. Larger organizations employing a range of staff may need more than one application form. Forms for relatively straightforward manual work can be kept simpler than the forms needed for more demanding professional and supervisory positions.

Selection

Selection is the final stage in the recruitment process, the stage when appointment to the job is decided. Such an important decision should be made in as objective a manner as possible, and a range of techniques exists for assisting in this process.

Unfortunately, in most organizations selection is traditionally made on the basis of a brief interview conducted by a manager or supervisor untrained in interviewing or selection methods, frequently without the aid of a job specification. All the evidence agrees that this is a bad way of making selection decisions. It is bad because it is subjective, because the wrong decision is frequently made and because in the long run this is a costly way of employing people.[7]

Selection aims to appoint individuals to jobs who will be successful in carrying out those jobs, achieving performance targets and integrating with work teams in a manner which is cost effective, legal and does not discriminate unfairly. As a rule of thumb there are four criteria which any good selection process should satisfy. These criteria – validity, reliability, acceptability and cost effectiveness – are examined below.

Criteria for selection methods

Validity

Validity is a simple concept which accords with common sense, although determining validity may be quite a complex operation. Validity measures the extent to which a selection procedure actually achieves success in predicting the competence of the individual in the job. The starting point for assessing validity is the job itself. First

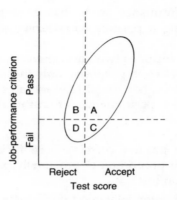

Figure 3.4 Scatter diagram showing correlation between selection test results and job performance

of all, criteria have to be established as to what constitutes successful performance on the job. This is an issue which is, of course, far wider than selection itself, and is basically to do with how work is managed. In well-managed organizations all positions have criteria for performance. In reality, very many organizations have not as yet established clear criteria for performance, a point taken up again in the next chapter in the context of performance management.

The next stage is to introduce measurement into the selection method or methods, measurement of performance by candidates for employment during the selection stage. Performance on paper and pencil tests is relatively easy to measure, performance during an employment interview is relatively difficult. But measurement is essential if validity is going to be established.

A simple way of demonstrating validity in statistical terms is provided by a graph on which performance in the selection method and performance subsequently in the job are plotted, as in Figure 3.4. If the selection method is valid, we would expect to see those scoring higher in the selection method performing better on the job than those recording lower scores. Correlation between any two measures, such as test results and job performance, can be stated in statistical terms. By statistical convention a perfect positive correlation is recorded as +1, a perfect negative correlation as −1, and no evidence of correlation as 0. Therefore, what we look for is a positive correlation of a relatively high order, e.g. +0.6 or +0.7, indicating a high degree of success in predicting performance. The relevance of this calculation is illustrated graphically in Figure 3.4, where a range of test and job-performance scores has been plotted as a scatter diagram, establishing a positive correlation coefficient of approximately +0.7.

The diagram also includes two lines: the vertical line indicates the present cut-off for selection purposes, only those reaching this score being selected, and the horizontal line indicates what is seen as an acceptable level of job performance. From this the following points can be observed:

1. Even as high a positive correlation coefficient as +0.7 means that a significant proportion of potentially poor performers may pass the selection test.
2. A proportion of potentially good performers may fail the test.
3. The employer can vary the level of test performance demanded of applicants, depending on how many recruits are required and how many potential failures on the job he can risk taking on.

Establishing the validity of a selection method can therefore be quite a complex business. Selection methods purveyed by reputable organizations will have already been validated for selected population groups (reputable lists of suppliers can be obtained from organizations such as the British Psychological Society and the Institute of Personnel Management). However, this does not obviate the need to carry out studies in one's own organization, because every organization is different, employs a different sample of people and sets its own criteria for job performance.

There are different types of validity, depending on the method used to try to establish validity, including:

1. *Predictive validity.* This means establishing, in the manner described above, whether a selection method predicts future performance. However, this can only be measured properly in a company taking on a large number of employees. It also involves not rejecting employees at the outset simply on account of their performance in the test, in order to permit proper follow-up studies on all applicants. Although this is the ideal type of validity for selection purposes, it is really only available to large organizations employing properly trained staff.
2. *Concurrent validity.* Tests are administered to existing employees, and the correlation between their current job performance and test performance is calculated. This tells us whether the test is valid for this sample of current employees, but does not

guarantee that it will be equally valid for a different group of people, namely new applicants. There may also be problems in overcoming trade-union resistance to testing of existing employees.

3. *Content validity*. Content validity measures the extent to which a test actually measures some aspect of the job itself, or has content similar to the job content. The more closely a selection test calls for performance which is similar to actual job performances, the better we are able to predict job performance from test performance. A case in point might be a typing test for a would-be typist.

4. *Face validity*. This is the appearance a test may give of being similar or related to a task, and is related to content validity. However, it represents a form of validity we must be very careful about because it is essentially subjective. A case in point might be the assumption that because a job involves stress, the manner in which individuals might cope with stress on the job can be predicted by introducing stress into the selection process, e.g. by use of a 'stress interview'. Evidence indicates that face validity can frequently be misleading and is no substitute for proper follow-up studies.

Reliability

A selection method may predict with accuracy one day, yet not be so accurate on another. Therefore we want to be confident that our selection methods can be trusted to come up with similar results day after day and week after week. Again, if selection tests are purchased from a reliable test agency, they should have been checked for reliability. Selection methods devised within an organization should be checked for reliability. Again, this can only be done by follow-up studies over a period of time.

Acceptability

Selection methods should be acceptable to all interested parties – applicants, selectors and senior managers. Under this heading also comes conformance to professional codes of practice and government legislation. Therefore, selection methods must be fair and seen to be fair. By way of illustration, here are some examples:

- *Racial discrimination and equal opportunities*: selection methods must satisfy current legislation, and not discriminate on grounds of race or sex.
- *Professional codes of practice*: certain forms of testing, particularly psychometric testing, must conform to the code of practice of the issuing body, which covers both the administration and the interpretation of the test.
- *Courtesy and good manners*: courtesy and good manners should be practised during the administration of selection procedures. As well as being morally right, this enhances the company's reputation as an employer. An example of bad practice is the way in which some organizations do not acknowledge receipt of applications.

Note: the Institute of Personnel Management has issued useful codes on occupational testing and on recruitment.

Cost effectiveness

Selection costs money. Bad selection frequently costs more, much more, than good selection. Nevertheless, there is a limit to what the organization can budget for. Therefore value for money must be a criterion.

To achieve all-round cost effectiveness one should examine employment procedures both collectively and singly. The reason for this in the context of selection is that the training of new recruits can modify the effects of selection policies. Likewise, other employment policies, such as pay systems or induction procedures, can either motivate or demotivate new recruits. It is of little benefit applying the very best selection procedures if what follows is counterproductive. Therefore budgets should be looked at in holistic fashion in the first instance.

Following this, one can cost the selection process itself and then weigh the evidence. Is the use of an expensive test leading to better selection, and is this, in turn, leading to higher productivity? There may be times when such money as is available would be better spent on improved training. Improving selection procedures and recruiting higher-calibre starters can lead to higher labour turnover unless induction and training are also improved in a manner that satisfies the new employees' higher expectations.

Having examined the four criteria for selection methods, we now turn to a brief description and review of the principal selection methods available. These are interviewing, psychometric tests (including intelligence and personality tests), references, biodata, ability tests and assessment centres.

Interviewing

We start with interviewing because it is the most widely used selection technique. Many employers perceive it as a relatively inexpensive and practical way of making employment decisions. They are frequently wrong. This is not because interviewing candidates itself is wrong, but because the manner in which the interviewing is carried out can be wrong. As already indicated, employment interviews by untrained managers and supervisors lead to very subjective judgements. It is no use trying to abolish interviewing, as some psychologists would have us do. So what can be done?

- Ensure all interviewers are properly trained. This means more than half a day of training. Several days of training using closed-circuit television and coaching are required.
- Ensure that job specifications are drawn up in advance, and are used as a framework for the interview.
- Ensure that application forms have been completed prior to the interview, and matched against the job specification.
- Ensure that employment decisions are not made solely on the basis of what happens in the employment interview.
- Supplement the information gained in the interview wherever possible with the results of aptitude and ability tests.

There is evidence that some people make better interviewers and make better employment decisions than others. We would expect this because of the manner in which abilities are distributed in the population. Unfortunately, most managers would be affronted if they were not held to be suitable as interviewers. But it would pay large organizations to determine which of their managers is making the more valid and reliable employment decisions.

Interviewing is a social process, and to be effective requires interpersonal skills. It also needs to follow some simple basic rules if both employer and potential employee are to feel satisfied. These include:

- Adequate preparation. Application forms need to be studied. The job specification should be issued to applicants well in advance.
- The venue should be adequate. This means using a comfortable room free from interruptions.
- Open-ended questions which require more than a 'yes' or 'no' answer should be asked on points relevant to the job.
- The interview should not be rushed. Adequate time should be allocated.
- The interviewee should have an opportunity to ask questions and to talk freely.

If panel interviews are used, then all members of the panel should be trained in panel interviewing, and the questioning should be planned and co-ordinated. Panel interviews are popular for public-sector appointments, and are favoured for political reasons. In fact, there is little evidence that they make good decisions, and therefore they must remain suspect as a selection device.

Intelligence tests

All jobs require some intelligence. Some jobs require very high levels of intelligence. Different jobs may require different types of intelligence. Therefore there is a case for testing intelligence where it can be shown that there is a high correlation between a particular type and level of intelligence and job performance.

Intelligence testing has attracted its share of controversy. There has been dispute as to whether it is an inherited aptitude, or whether it can be nurtured; how many types of intelligence exist, whether there is a basic underlying dimension of intelligence common to all these types and whether it can be measured. This is not the place to examine all these issues, some of which have social and political connotations. From a practical managerial perspective the important question is, does it work? The evidence is that it does work in certain situations and for certain jobs.[8] However, for social

Look at the six figures. Four of them are alike in some way, but two do not belong with the other four. For each question decide which two figures do not belong with the other four. Mark your answers in the Answers boxes.

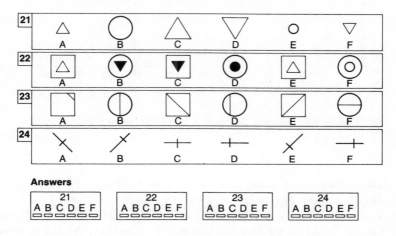

Figure 3.5 Example of a problem-solving test of intelligence

and practical reasons intelligence testing tends to be used only for the selection of junior employees. Reasons for this include the reluctance of older employees to undertake tests and the absence of a career history for younger employees on which to base selection decisions, making the results of intelligence tests particularly useful in their case.

Two types, or facets, of intelligence have been found to be particularly useful for selection purposes. These are numerical ability and verbal ability. Some individuals are stronger on one than the other, some are strong or weak on both. Intelligence tests frequently take the form of tests of convergent reasoning ability, the ability to apply logical solutions to problems that have only one correct answer. These problems usually involve numbers and/or patterns. As well as their demonstrated usefulness, there exists a strong argument that such problem solving is 'culture fair' in a way that verbal tests are not. That is to say, they do not discriminate by ethnic background, and do not require understanding of a particular language. Examples of typical problems are provided in Figure 3.5. However, there are many work situations where convergent thinking is not relevant, as in creative work and, indeed, a lot of managerial work.

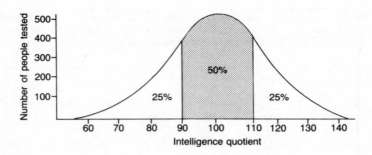

Figure 3.6 Normal distribution curve for general intelligence

The notion of IQ is frequently used in everyday speech. IQ, or intelligence quotient, was a term originally conceived of as a measure of a child's development of intelligence during the formative years. It was used as a relative term, measuring the relationship between a child's capacity to perform in intelligence tests compared with other children. A child of 12 who performed at the same level as the average for 14-year-old children could be said to have an IQ of:

$$\frac{14}{12} \times 100 = 117.$$

However, these days IQ is frequently applied to adults, usually by making it relative to the normal curve of distribution for a large sample of the population to whom intelligence tests have been administered.

Figure 3.6 shows a typical normal curve of distribution of intelligence in the population, and, added to it, a corresponding IQ scale. A normal curve of distribution is a statistical method of describing a universal phenomenon, namely the fact that certain human attributes, such as height, weight and in this case intelligence, are distributed in the population in the manner described by the curve. A significant proportion of the population are 'about average', while progressively smaller proportions are above and below average.

Should the job specification call for a certain level of intelligence, then it is worth investigating the use of intelligence tests. As with all the tests referred to in this chapter it is important to deal only with reputable agencies.

Personality tests

While most people will agree that personality is a very important factor in contributing to success or failure on the job, there is far less agreement on the nature of personality and how it should be measured. Once again, we must adopt a pragmatic managerial approach. Do personality tests work?

The evidence is that, yes, they do work up to a point, and if administered only by carefully selected and trained individuals. That is to say, certain tests produced by reputable organizations do measure, with a fair degree of consistency, certain personality traits, and there is evidence in a number of cases that certain personality traits correlate with successful performance on the job. However, these correlations are frequently disappointingly small.

Two of the most frequently used and reliable personality tests in the United Kingdom have been developed by well-known occupational psychologists, namely Cattell, and Saville and Holdsworth. Cattell's test is termed the 16PF, because it purports to measure sixteen personality factors which can then be used to 'profile' an individual in the manner shown in Figure 3.7. The test was developed in the United States, but British versions are available. The test devised by Saville and Holdsworth is termed the OPQ (occupational personality questionnaire) and comes in a number of different forms. It has been standardized for British populations, and an outline is provided in Figure 3.8.

Because of the obvious dangers of misapplication and misinterpretation, personality tests must also come from reliable sources and be applied by trained testers. If in doubt, managers are advised to contact the British Psychological Society or the Institute of Personnel Management.

References

It is the practice of many organizations to take up references on candidates. In certain cases, as where matters of national security, child protection, medical practice or high financial probity are concerned, references are necessary. However, the evidence is that in many cases references for routine positions are largely a waste of time and are open to abuse.[9] Employers may be unwilling to provide

	Low meaning	16 PF profile	High meaning
		1 2 3 4 5 6 7 8 9 10	
A 9	Reserved	*	Warm–friendly
B 9	Less intelligent	*	More intelligent
C 7	Affected by feelings	*	Calm–unruffled
E 7	Not assertive	*	Dominant
F 5	Reflective-serious	*	Active (?impulse)
G 4	Expedient	*	Conscientious
H 7	Shy	*	Socially venturesome
I 4	Tough-minded–objective	*	Tender-minded–subjective
L 7	Trusting	*	Suspicious
M 5	Practical	*	Imaginative
N 5	Forthright	*	Shrewd
O 6	Confident	*	Apprehensive
Q1 7	Conservative	*	Experimenting
Q2 8	Group-oriented	*	Self-sufficient
Q3 6	Undisciplined	*	Self-disciplined
Q4 3	Relaxed	*	Tense

Broad patterns
Extraversion is 5.7 average
Tough poise is 4.3 below average
Independence is 7.9 high
Dependability is 4.1 below average
Accident-error proneness is predicted to be 5.0 average
Potential to learn from on-the-job experience is 7.1 above average
Potential to profit from formal academic training is 7.5 high
Creativity and inventiveness are estimated to be 6.7 above average
Leadership potential is 6.6 above average

Figure 3.7   A Cattell 16PF personality profile

references, or only to answer certain questions, such as dates of employment. Many references are not valid or reliable predictors of performance. The best advice is to use them only if you have to, and treat them with caution.

Biodata

'Biodata' is a term used to describe the use of biographical data to predict success in a job. It has both a general application and specific applications in the form of particular techniques.

Its general application is based on the recognition that behaviour in the past helps to predict behaviour in the future. Most individuals are reasonably consistent in their behaviour over time. Therefore if

Relationships with people

Assertive	Persuasive	Enjoys selling, changes opinions of others, convincing with arguments, negotiates
	Controlling	Takes charge, directs, manages, organizes, supervises others
	Independent	Has strong views on things, difficult to manage, speaks up, argues, dislikes ties
Gregarious	Outgoing	Fun loving, humorous, sociable, vibrant, talkative, jovial
	Affiliative	Has many friends, enjoys being in groups, likes companionship, shares things with friends
	Socially confident	Puts people at ease, knows what to say, good with words
Empathy	Modest	Reserved about achievements, avoids talking about self, accepts others, avoids trappings of status
	Democratic	Encourages others to contribute, consults, listens and refers to others
	Caring	Considerate to others, helps those in need, sympathetic, tolerant

The OPQ concept model consists of five questionnaires which each measure thirty personality dimensions. The concept model also forms the basis for the OPQ applications: team types, leadership and subordinate styles and selling influencing styles. The concept model also has a computer-based expert system available for interpreting the OPQ.

Figure 3.8 Saville and Holdsworth occupational personality questionnaire. The concept model, an example of a personality dimension

we know enough about their life history, we can make predictions about future behaviour, and this can greatly assist in job selection. First, however, we need to decide, on the basis of job specification, what kind of individuals are likely to be most successful on the job. This requires a study of the kinds of people who are successful in the job at the present time. An American study of employees in a clothing factory, for example, found that long-tenure employees tended to be aged between 30 and 39, had children under the age of 6, had at least three years' prior work experience and had spent no more than nine years in formal education.[10]

Specific applications include WABs (weighted inventory blanks) and BIBs (biographical information blanks). The WAB is a technique for scoring an application form, where items are weighted. Completed application forms can then be scored, and the scores used to short list applicants for the job. Biographical information blanks are specifically designed biodata forms, which standardize the data to be collected and the means of collecting it, and then replace the subjective criteria of the interview by weighting each piece of information with a clear scoring system tailored to the position to be filled.

The disadvantages of biodata include the cost and time required for studies to determine the critical biographical issues. The advantages include evidence that it is relatively objective and can improve selection. But probably the most important point is the reminder it provides to managers making selection decisions that the systematic collection of biographical information about candidates, using application forms and structured interviews in conjunction with job specifications, can make for better employment decisions.

Ability tests

In many ways the ideal selection method is simply to start prospective employees on the job, and see how they get on. Those who are successful can be retained, and those who fail can be fired. Unfortunately life is not that simple. It is usually too disruptive to start potentially unsuitable employees, and is not easy to fire them. Additionally, some of the failures might have been successful had they been trained properly after hiring.

Ability testing aims to test the applicant's ability to perform the job by making tests as similar to the task as possible. A potential secretary may be asked to undergo a typewriting test. This tests typing skills, and is normally a good predictor of typing performance in the job, although a good secretary requires a far greater range of skills than just typing. In a modern British car factory, job applicants take tests covering welding, machining, fork-lift truck driving, handling tools and reading drawings.[11]

Ability tests have much to recommend them and, if well designed, achieve higher predictive levels than paper and pencil type tests.

Assessment centres

Individual selection methods used by themselves are not good predictors of performance. However, if used in combination, the chances of making a good selection are considerably increased. Assessment centres make use of a range of selection devices in order to improve selection decisions, but in consequence take time (normally two to three days) and cost a lot of money. They are therefore normally used only by large organizations needing to make important employment decisions for key categories of staff. This usually means the selection of staff for management training, or for graduate recruitment.

Assessment centres test small groups of participants using a series of tests and exercises conducted under observation. Methods used include psychometric tests, interviews and job simulation exercises. The job simulation exercises may include group discussion, in-tray exercises, problem-solving and role-playing exercises. Performance in the exercises is judged by trained observers, many of whom are drawn from the ranks of line managers.

As in all forms of selection, job specifications and the desired competencies need to have been determined in advance, and the process needs to be monitored and validated. The expense can be justified if it ensures a continuous flow of good people into management training programmes and produces good candidates for promotion. A further benefit is that feedback and counselling can be provided to internal participants to assist them in developing greater competence.

References

1. Olins, R. (ed.), 'Polishing up the image in the skills crisis', *Sunday Times*, 5 November 1989.
2. Jones, T., 'Managers "wrong pay"', *The Times*, 17 May 1989.
3. Whitehill, A. M., *Japanese Management*, London: Routledge, 1991.
4. Cowling, A. and Mailer, C., *Managing Human Resources* (2nd edn), Sevenoaks, England: Edward Arnold, 1990, pp. 14–15.
5. Mitrani, A., Dalziel, M. and Fih, D., *Competency Based Human Resource Management*, London: Kogan Page, 1992.
6. Wheeler, D., 'How to recruit a recruitment agency', *Personnel Management*, April 1988.

7.   Bevan, S. and Fryatt, J., *Employee Selection in the UK*, Institute of Manpower Studies Report 160, December 1988.
8.   Kline, P., *Intelligence, the psychometric view*, London: Routledge, 1991, Ch. 5.
9.   Anderson, N. and Shackleton, V., 'Recruitment and selection: a review of developments in the 1980s', *Personnel Review*, **15**, 1986, p. 4.
10. Strebler, M., *Biodata in Selection: issues in practice*, Institute of Manpower Studies Paper No. 160, January 1991.
11. IDS Study, *Recruiting Manual Workers*, Study 433, Incomes Data Services Ltd, May 1989.

4
Motivation and reward management

Motivating staff has always been one of the biggest challenges facing employers. This is especially so today when the winning formula is 'performance through people'. Yet too many attitude surveys conducted within companies indicate that staff are not fully motivated, do not have confidence in their leadership and feel that the old bonds of loyalty have broken down. Employers may point to low rates of turnover as an indication of staff satisfaction, conveniently forgetting that high levels of unemployment pressurize staff into staying in their jobs whether or not they choose to do so. The overriding objective for employers has to be high all-round performance. This will be delivered only by staff who are positively motivated, having a high level of commitment to what they are doing. Good personnel management aims to bring about high levels of commitment. Motivation and the intelligent management of rewards provide the means.

Reward management should be a positive means to achieving high levels of motivation. But consider the terms that have been used to describe and execute this process. British companies and British textbooks still use words such as 'wages' and 'salaries' to describe their reward systems. This demonstrates a hangover from the worst days of class distinction at work when blue-collar manual workers earned wages, whereas white-collar office workers were given salaries. Many American companies still use the term 'compensation', implying that work is such a negative experience employees have to be 'compensated' for turning up!

Another negative attitude to reward management dies hard. This is cost accountants' approach, which sees wages merely as a cost.

Cost it certainly is, but that is an argument for using the money wisely, not for pushing for cost-cutting exercises that lower morale and motivation and hence productivity, a policy that, sooner or later, will impact negatively on the bottom line and the quality of service. High wages and high productivity lead to a lower *total* wage bill than a low-wage, low-productivity approach.

One further thought merits consideration before we examine in greater detail the principles and processes of motivation and reward management, and that is the missing link between pay and productivity in many large organizations. This arises from the bureaucratic nature of so many salary structures which are structured on the basis of a large range of incremental points. These schemes tend to reward length of service rather than performance. Members of staff sitting at adjoining desks may be doing similar jobs, but with one employee earning considerably more than the other employee, despite an inferior performance. For this reason a popular slogan amongst reformers today is 'Pay for contribution, do not pay for status.'[1]

Motivation

We are all motivated in pursuit of the goods that we desire. But we are not all motivated by our jobs. The challenge is to align individual and group goals with the goals of the organizations and, where appropriate, the goals of the organizations with the goals of individuals and groups.

Money is frequently seen as the primary factor in motivating people to work, and of course in many ways it is. But money is for most people a means to an end. We need money to survive in our society. Money derived from our pay packets purchases the living standards we aspire to. However, we all have 'trade offs' between maximizing our earnings and our desire for more leisure, greater security, more interesting work and career development. Good personnel management takes account of the variety of human needs in trying to ensure high levels of motivation and productivity.

There are three theories of motivation which are particularly relevant to motivating people in work situations and which we examine briefly below. These are Herzberg's so-called 'two factor' theory, Lawler's version of 'expectancy theory', and 'path–goal' theory.

•

Herzberg's original research into motivation was conducted over thirty years ago, but has been replicated on a number of occasions since, and still carries food for thought today. Based on individual responses to questions as to what provides them with the most memorable instances of happiness or unhappiness at work, people indicate two different lists of factors, one contributing to happiness, the other to unhappiness. Typically the former list includes:

- a sense of achievement;
- recognition by superiors;
- responsibility inherent in the job;
- a job content that is personally satisfying;
- promotion.

By way of contrast, the negative factors typically include the following:

- company policy and administration;
- relationships with supervisors and peers;
- physical working conditions.

In these surveys pay levels also attract considerable comment, some of a favourable nature, but more frequently unfavourable. This led Herzberg to dub the second list 'hygiene' factors, on the grounds that they need to be dealt with before positive motivation can take place, in much the same way as human beings have to observe the rules of hygiene before they can progress to high levels of physical fitness and performance.[2]

These findings led to the inference that pay does not motivate, and that employers should focus on achieving a well-administered pay system and erasing causes of dissatisfaction amongst employees, before moving on to the more exciting measures that create high levels of motivation and performance. Although there is a large measure of truth in this inference, and experience and research both tell us that it is extremely hard to motivate dissatisfied employees, it obscures the role that money can have in achieving high levels of motivation. The reasons for this are brought out in the next theory of motivation, examined below. However, for a significant proportion of employees, particularly high-flying managers and sales staff, high levels of financial reward are an important form of recognition. Money can become a goal in itself, as well as a reinforcing behaviour that leads to high performance.

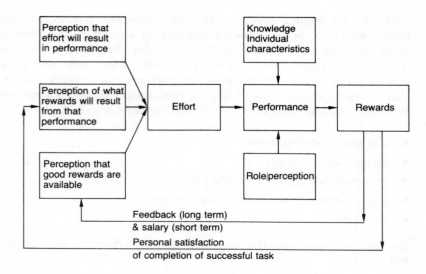

Figure 4.1   Expectancy theory of motivation and reward management – applied model

The second theory of motivation particularly relevant to reward management is expectancy theory.[3] This comes in a number of versions; the essence is portrayed in Figure 4.1. Expectancy theory concentrates, as the name implies, on the expectations that employees bring with them to the work situation, and the context and manner in which these expectations are satisfied. The underlying hypothesis is that appropriate levels of effort, and hence productivity, will be extended only if employees' expectations are fulfilled. It does not assume a static range of expectations common to all employees, but rather points to the possibility of different sets of expectations. Rewards are seen as fulfilling or not fulfilling expectations. The principal contribution that expectancy theory makes is to challenge management to prove that their employees actually perceive that extra effort will reap a commensurate reward. Regrettably, once again the evidence of research and practical experience is that very many employees are not convinced that if they exert more effort they will definitely achieve more and will definitely be rewarded accordingly. However, this can be rectified.

This link between effort and reward may encompass the pay packet as well as a variety of other extrinsic or intrinsic rewards. Proponents cite research evidence to show that money can motivate, and continue to motivate, a proportion of employees. Therefore reward schemes should create for appropriate sections of the work-force a positive link between the size of the pay packet and the effort expended. For others, links must be created between effort and rewards for their dominant needs, which may include factors already alluded to, such as job satisfaction, praise and other forms of recognition.

There is strong evidence that setting goals for employees leads to higher performance, provided the goals are relevant and acceptable to participants. Goal-setting theories, originally propounded by Locke, have considerable relevance to motivation and reward management.[4] At its most basic levels, this means that all employees should:

- be clear about their individual and group goals;
- participate in the setting of these goals.

Goal choice is a function of (1) what the individual expects can be achieved; (2) what the individual would ideally like to achieve; and (3) what the individual believes is the minimum that should be achieved. For many people, a goal set and delegated by others serves as a disincentive. For goals to have their full effect it is also necessary for participants to have feedback on whether their performance has been successful.

The most obvious applications of goal theory are in managerial style and the design of appraisal schemes. As management is a process of achieving results through people, successful managers will involve staff in goal setting ('management by objectives'), ensure that the goals can be achieved and provide feedback on whether goals are being achieved.[5] This contrasts with a proverbial saying in British industry that senior management are guided by the 'mushroom' theory of growth – 'keep staff in the dark and shower them with shit'! Unfortunately the 'mushroom' theory has, in too many cases, led to poor-quality results and contrasts sharply with the Japanese style of communication and consultation.

Reward management

Reward management is a relatively modern term describing the process of managing rewards within an organization for the purpose of supporting the purpose of the organization, in the most effective manner possible. It represents a stark contrast to traditional piecemeal approaches to pay that had just 'grown like Topsy' over a number of years. Pressures on employers to adopt a more modern approach include:

1. *Cost.* Competitive pressures have placed a spotlight on employment costs, leading employers to search for ways of achieving greater output with reduced expenditure on employment costs.
2. *Strategic vision.* The past decade has seen a growing realization that 'performance through people' is the only way to stay competitive and achieve quality service. This requires that rewards should be reviewed to ensure that they motivate employees to achieve high performance.
3. *New developments in theory and practice.* On the theoretical front, research findings by social scientists have pointed to the manner in which rewards can be used to motivate staff. On the practical side, a body of good practice and useful techniques has been developed within organizations by senior managers and consultants.

Reward management takes account of both 'extrinsic' and 'intrinsic' rewards. Extrinsic rewards are 'tangible' rewards such as cash, pensions, bonuses, holidays, status symbols, travel vouchers and the like. Intrinsic rewards are in the main psychological, and include job satisfaction, praise and recognition, pride in work and sense of achievement. This is why reward management is not just about the pay packet. Reward management recognizes that the objectives are high levels of productivity and good-quality working. These require good relationships, well-designed jobs, teamworking, and high levels of job satisfaction as well as a pay packet which is perceived as both fair and competitive.

Considerations of 'fairness' and 'competitiveness' are best examined in the context of the 'internal' and 'external' labour markets. These terms describe pressures on pay generated internally within organizations and pressures generated externally by the supply of, and demand for, people in the general market-place. But before we examine these in more detail, we need to set out the essential aims to be pursued in reward management. The basic aims of reward management are as follows:

●   To attract quality staff from the labour market.

- To retain good staff.
- To motivate staff.
- To control costs.

The rationale for these is reasonably self-evident. These basic aims provide a useful checklist for organizations. All too frequently, organizations satisfy some but not all of these aims and therefore run into serious problems.

Recruitment and selection are looked at in more detail in Chapter 3. Recruiting the right quality of staff helps to ensure the long-term survival and competitiveness of the organization. This means that rewards (i.e. the total reward package, including pay) must be attractive, which means, in turn, being competitive with other would-be employers. The retention of staff is also examined in more detail in Chapter 3. The impact on productivity of losing good staff to other employers can be considerable. A consistent approach to non-performers is also needed. This does not mean sacking staff as soon as their performance drops, but does mean finding out the causes and attempting to remedy the situation. Of course, it also means not ignoring poor performance, an attitude which has been surprisingly prevalent in some organizations in the past.

The control of costs should arise naturally from pressures to improve productivity. The cost of employing staff should constantly be weighed against the value of their contribution. The cost of employing staff encompasses not only their direct wage costs, but also the cost of indirect benefits, office space, equipment, overheads and the like.

Maintaining competitive rewards

At first sight, maintaining rewards at a competitive level might seem a straightforward business. Just find out what other employers are paying, and adjust your pay rates accordingly. In practice, life is more complicated.

Initially, a number of key policy decisions are required, and a number of questions have to be answered:

- What can we afford now, and in the near future?
- From which sections of the economy, and from what parts of the country (or other countries) do we draw our staff?

- Do we attract applicants principally through the size of the pay packets we offer, or through our reputation and good working conditions – or a combination of both?

- Is it our policy to be a 'pay leader', or to be within the top 25 per cent of employers – or to be just 'average'?

The relevance of the geographical location of existing employees and potential employees was examined in Chapter 2. If we aim to attract and retain, say, information technology (IT) staff and we are located in an industrial city in the Midlands, it is important to know where existing employees with these skills and the pool of potential employees live. We also need to know which other employers are competing in the same 'pool'.

Whether we choose to be a pay leader or not will depend on whether we aim to recruit and retain only the very best staff, or whether we are confident that we can still achieve our goals with more 'ordinary' staff. It is usually a bad mistake to recruit staff at salary levels higher than those of existing staff because when the latter get to know about it, as they surely will in time, there will be considerable bad feeling.

There is a variety of sources of information about the levels of pay and conditions offered by other employers competing in our labour markets, including:

- Incomes data services from specialist consultancy and journal sources.

- Pay survey 'clubs' of employers, which exchange information on pay rates at regular intervals.

- 'One-off' surveys by personnel departments questioning their opposite numbers in other organizations.

- Official statistics from government sources and Job Centres.

- Information collected in the course of interviewing job applicants and from job adverts in the press.

But before data are gathered, a preliminary step is essential, i.e. ensuring that job descriptions are available. Like must be compared with like. It is very misleading just to go on job title. Systematic pay surveys yield the best results, because they are based on accurate job descriptions. A good survey involving a number of employers should also produce useful statistical data, showing the average rates of pay and conditions for specific jobs, the range and the upper and lower quartiles.

Official government statistics on pay and pay trends and the retail price index are also useful, particularly when negotiating with trade unions. Unfortunately, these have limitations because they are usually several months out of date by the time they are published.

Achieving internal equity based on job content

Most people at work have a strong sense of what is a fair rate of pay, and what is not. This is based on their knowledge of what their fellow workers are being paid. If staff do not feel fairly treated, then they are unlikely to give of their best. At the same time, it is useful to have an orderly structure of pay rates within a company.

The traditional solution to these requirements has been to create a direct link between rates of pay and the content of the job. The more complex and demanding the job, the greater the level of pay. The term used to describe this system of relative pay values is 'job evaluation'.

Job evaluation has been practised in one form or another in Western industrialized nations for over seventy years. Fundamental to job evaluation are job descriptions. The process of writing job descriptions was described in Chapter 3. Job descriptions can be used to establish a rational hierarchy of pay, based on a demonstrable relationship between job content and pay. This of course begs the question as to whether managers and workers might have different views as to what that relationship should be.

There are four standard versions of job evaluation. The first two are termed 'ranking' and 'grading' (or classification), and are considered to be 'non-analytical' because they do not analyze the jobs under factor headings. The ranking method requires that those doing the job evaluation place all the jobs in rank order, from lowest to highest, and the pay levels are then adjusted accordingly. This is not difficult to do with a few jobs, but becomes difficult when there are a lot of jobs to be evaluated. Grading (or classification) describes a pay structure where the number of grades is predetermined. There may, for example, be six grades, and jobs are then allocated to their respective grades based on judgements about the content of the jobs. This is a technique that has recently come back into favour as organizations have chosen to reduce the number of layers in their structures, although paradoxically it has long been favoured by old-fashioned bureaucracies, embodying anything up to twenty

Points table

Factor number	Factors	%	Minimum points	Degree			
				1	2	3	4
1	Staff responsibility	16.66	166.6	267	367	467	567
2	Financial responsibility	16.66	166.6	267	367	467	567
3	Information/records responsibility	16.66	166.6	267	367	467	567
4	Communications	16.66	166.6	267	367	467	567
5	Complexity	16.66	166.6	267	367	467	567
6	Decision making and judgement	16.66	166.6	267	367	467	567
	Total	99.96	1000	1600	2200	2800	3400

Grade bandings

Grade 1   1000–1280 points
Grade 2   1281–1560 points
Grade 3   1561–1840 points
Grade 4   1841–2120 points
Grade 5   2121–2400 points
Grade 6   2401–2680 points
Grade 7   2681–2960 points
Grade 8   2961–3400 points

Figure 4.2 Job evaluation – an example of a points system and grade-bandings structure

grades (or 'classifications') in their structures. Administering a very large number of grades can, of course, be very time consuming.

The two analytical methods are conventionally termed 'factor comparison' and 'points method'. In both cases jobs are analyzed under factor headings such as 'responsibility', 'training and experience required' and 'relationships'. Ranking takes place under each factor heading. The problem of how to translate this into money terms is neatly solved by the 'points' method, allocating a range of points to each factor. The scores achieved by a particular job under each factor are then added up, and converted into pay. An example is provided in Figure 4.2, taken from a public-sector organization. It

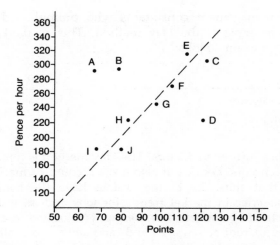

Figure 4.3 Job evaluation – a scattergram of points and money

will be seen from this example that critical decisions for management include the factors to be used, the range of points to be
allocated to each factor (i.e. their 'weighting') and, of course, just
who allocates the points. Sometimes allocation of points is the sole
prerogative of management, sometimes a joint management–worker
committee is set up.

The points method of job evaluation is, in practice, a superstruc-
ture based on a foundation of so-called 'bench-mark' jobs. Bench-
mark jobs are a small number of jobs that cover the range of jobs to
be evaluated, which are felt by the evaluators to demonstrate a
correct relationship between job content and pay. Once the bench-
mark jobs have been agreed, all other jobs can be evaluated. Some
will be found to be out of line because they are paid too much or too
little in relation to their job content, and they are therefore brought
into line. However, a guarantee is frequently given in advance to
individuals that no one will have their personal pay levels reduced
even if job rates are cut, although new incumbents to the job will
start at the new correct rate. This process is demonstrated graphically in Figure 4.3.

In recent years a variety of hybrid forms of job evaluation have
been developed that place particular emphasis on certain aspects of
the evaluation. For example, the so-called 'consensus' method
places emphasis on achieving consensus amongst employees on the
grades to be allocated. Sometimes these methods are named after

the firm of management consultants who promulgated them. A well-known example is the Hay method. This method uses just three factors to evaluate jobs:

- know how;
- problem solving;
- accountability;

Each factor has further subfactors. The Hay method is not a pure job evaluation technique because it also takes account of market forces. Companies that subscribe to the system have the benefit of an information service in market trends for jobs and an indication of what value should be attached to the points allocated to each job.

For all its apparent advantages and rationality, job evaluation has been fiercely criticized, and some companies have stopped using it. A major criticism used to be that it reinforced discrimination, particularly sexual discrimination, in the labour force. This was because heavier weightings were seen to be given to factors favouring men, such as strength or apprenticeship training, whereas factors covering such skills as dexterity or caring, which featured in women's work, were given a low weighting. This situation has now been largely rectified. Job evaluation finds favour with many industrial tribunals because it creates a payment system that is open to external inspection and correction.

The most serious criticism of job evaluation arises from its bureaucratic nature.[6] Because it is based on job description, it assumes a degree of stability and hierarchy that is increasingly unrealistic in a world of rapid change. Organizations today have to be flexible and responsive, and this means that staff must accept that their jobs are also susceptible to rapid change. Demarcation of jobs is out and flexibility is in, in today's world. Furthermore, it is felt by many organizations that external market conditions are of greater significance that internal relativities and, as we shall be examining later, teamworking requires different forms of payment. It is as well, therefore, to remind ourselves more of the principle expressed on a number of occasions in 'this book – there are no 'right' and 'wrong' personnel management techniques, only techniques that are more or less appropriate to organizations at any given time. However, at the end of the day, pay systems have to bear some relationship to the content of jobs or the whole structure becomes indefensible, although, as we shall see below, this can be achieved without relying exclusively on job evaluation.

Payment by results

Payment by results (PBR) is a traditional method of linking the level of pay to quantity of output of individuals or groups of workers. It has been particularly associated with manual work, where the physical output can be measured. An earlier version of PBR was termed 'piecework', where money was given for the number of pieces of work completed by a worker. Piecework was frequently used to pay garment workers, for example.

Payment by results has found favour with many employers for more than eighty years, and is supported by some strong arguments. The first is to do with motivation, and is the argument that the opportunity to earn more money will lead to harder work and higher output. The second is fairness. It is 'fair' that those who produce more should earn more. The third is cost. Workers on PBR, it is assumed, will require less supervision, and the costs of production will be held down as wages are linked to output.

Payment by results in well-managed firms has frequently been controlled by work-study engineers. Trained work-study engineers decide on the best method of doing the job by means of 'method-study' techniques, and rates of pay are then set by 'effort-rating'. In effort-rating the work-study engineer calculates the time taken to complete tasks by a worker working at the correct speed (i.e. exerting the appropriate amount of 'effort'), and the worker is paid according to his or her output. In order to systematize this, a number of scales have been developed, linking pay to output. A good example is provided by the British Standards Institution (BSI) 100 scale. Put simply, this assumes that a worker on PBR should be able to earn one-third more than a worker on a so-called 'time rate' (i.e. a worker paid by the hour, irrespective of output) if working at the correct speed. If a rate has been negotiated for a timeworker, say for £3 an hour, then a PBR worker exerting the appropriate amount of effort should be able to earn £4 an hour. In practice, of course, one would anticipate that some workers would earn less and some earn more, assuming some individuals are faster and more hard-working than others.

It is possible for companies to vary the relationship between output and rewards for different levels of output in a manner which helps them to achieve production targets. They may wish, for example, to encourage workers to work particularly hard up to a certain level of output, but then to begin to ease off. This process of linking pay and output is shown graphically in Figure 4.4.

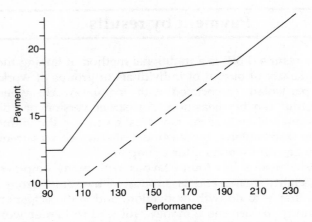

Figure 4.4 Example of a variable PBR system based on BSI ratings

As with all management techniques, there are arguments both in favour and against, and once again we have to consider what is best in a particular situation. Payment by results can accentuate hostility between management and workers when PBR is seen as a management tool to extort more work out of workers, and when workers feel that work is being devalued to a series of hostile negotiations over money for effort. Added to this are genuine problems of measuring effort, and the risk that pressure for output will lead to poor-quality work and a neglect of health and safety standards. Payment by results also provides an opportunity for trade unions to demonstrate their support for their members by constantly arguing the toss over rates of pay, as well as providing an opportunity for workers to devote their energies to outwitting management and work-study engineers rather than getting on with the job. The available evidence indicates that PBR can work where the scheme is well thought out, when working methods lend themselves to measurement, where industrial relations are good, and where high levels of communication and consultation take place before schemes are introduced.[7]

Appraisal

Appraisal is considered in this chapter in the context of reward management, although appraisal also has a significant role in training and development and career planning, as well as being at the heart of much good management practice.

Most of us are familiar with appraisal in one form or another. Even if we are not subject to formalized in-company appraisal schemes, we are aware that we are being appraised informally by our superiors, which means that judgements are continuously being made about our performance. The principal argument in favour of formalized appraisal schemes is that they place this process of subjective judgement on to a more objective basis that is open to scrutiny. The principal argument against formalized appraisal schemes is that a high proportion have failed to meet their objectives, and in the process have alienated both staff and management. Nevertheless, it is possible to develop appraisal schemes that make a really useful contribution to the objectives of the organization, reward good performers, help all staff to do better and enhance the personal sense of achievement of staff and management. The relevant considerations and stages to achieving this are described below.

First, be clear about the aims of the appraisal scheme. Is it aiming to improve current performance, or to ascertain staff development needs or to reward high performers? No system can achieve all these aims simultaneously. But the biggest mistake is to think that the introduction of an appraisal scheme will rectify serious defects in the manner in which the organization is managed. Therefore before introducing formal appraisal an audit of management should be carried out. Has the organization a clear mission and a well-thought-out corporate strategy? Has it communicated these to staff? Are managers well trained? Do attitude surveys indicate a high level of job satisfaction?

Secondly, having satisfied these preliminary considerations, decide how formalized the appraisal scheme needs to be. The critical question here is the extent to which the organization needs to be run on bureaucratic or decentralized lines. A bureaucratic, hierarchical structured organization will require a highly formalized appraisal system based on well-defined job descriptions. However, as has been made clear throughout this book, very few organizations these days can afford to be bureaucratic, because bureaucracies cannot adapt easily to change, and for most organizations the environment is undergoing rapid change. Therefore most organizations will require appraisal systems that are simple, flexible and easy to operate.

The third consideration is just what is to be appraised. The evidence from research and experience is that the primary focus should be on the achievement of results, and not on personality traits. Individuals can do very little to change their personalities, but they can do a lot about improving their performance. This indicates that appraisal forms should contain space for a statement of what results are to be aimed for, and whether they are being achieved.

The fourth consideration is how to measure or 'appraise' performance. This requires that realistic quantifiable targets should be built in with specific time spans for their achievement. Measurement then becomes measurement of the extent to which results are achieved by a due date.

The fifth consideration is participation. To what extent should subordinates participate in the setting of performance aims? The evidence is that, other things being equal, the more individuals genuinely participate in the setting of goals, the more committed they are to achieving them, and therefore the more likely they are to improve their performance.

The sixth consideration is training. Many managers do not find appraisal an easy thing to carry out, and may lack the skills to conduct appraisal interviews. An appropriate investment in training is essential.

The seventh consideration is timing. Should appraisals be once a year, or more frequent? Traditionally they have been conducted once a year in order to coincide with the annual salary review, which in turn was linked to the financial year. But a one-year cycle is rarely appropriate to work tasks. Work tasks may have one-month, six-month or two-year natural cycles from start or finish, or something in between. Therefore it may be right to conduct appraisals ('performance reviews') on any day in the year that marks the conclusion of relevant tasks or projects.

Finally, the appraisal scheme must be 'owned' by those who operate it. A scheme foisted onto managers by the personnel department will not work if it is not perceived as being helpful. This calls for considerable consultation and delegation, while, at the same time, a monitoring procedure to ensure that it is happening must be in place.[8,9]

The essence of a good appraisal system is shown in Figure 4.5.

Pay for skills and competence

Traditionally, skilled workers have been paid more than their less skilled fellow workers. However, this approach has taken a com-

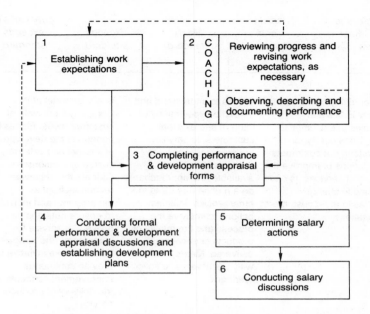

Source: Gomez-Mejia, L. R., Page, R. C. and Tornow, W. W., 'Improving the effectiveness of performance appraisal', *Personnel Administrator*, Jauary 1985.

Figure 4.5 Appraisal as a system linking work performance, pay and development

pletely new angle in the contemporary situation. This is because of the pace of change already alluded to, which means that organizations are constantly having to develop new ways of working.[10] Until the 1970s the general trend in the industrial Western nations was towards work simplification and deskilling, a logical extension to assembly-line production. However, new technology means that unskilled jobs are disappearing rapidly and there is now an emphasis on quality, teamworking and adaptability. This in turn requires new skills. In order to acquire a work-force with appropriate skills, employers are, in some cases, linking rewards directly to the acquisition of relevant skills. This requires that the amount of money attached to the acquisition and demonstration of a relevant skill should be sufficient to encourage the process.

Skills base pay (SBP) is a rewards system based on the acquisition of skills and knowledge, and is on the increase in both the manufacturing and service sectors. Experience to date indicates that it is not suitable for all situations, requires careful planning, and

Fails to meet standard	Partially meets standard	Meets standard	Exceeds standard	Substantially exceeds standard

Not genuinely committed to equality ideals and principles of customer focus. Does not try to understand our customers' expectations or improve the delivery of services. Is often unwilling to change priorities to meet customers' expectations.

Strives to understand and meet the expectations of internal and external customers. Is service-oriented: responsive to requests from others, available and approachable on a routine basis and in emergencies. Initiates actions to improve the process and the quality of products or services delivered. Meets frequently with customers and solicits feedback.

Is a role model of the Company's principle of customer focus. Places high priority on the development of internal and external customer relationships. Gathers the necessary resources from all departments and individuals to ensure outstanding delivery of service to customers. Encourages others to take initiative to provide continuous improvement concepts to the delivery of products and services.

Figure 4.6 Competencies and customer services – example from a typical company handbook

needs to be preceded by a more participative and open system of working. Significant resources need to be devoted to training, which includes training in new skills and in teamworking. Rewards need to be linked not only to the acquisition of skills but to their application, and possibly also to the performance achieved.[11]

Competency has been defined as 'an underlying characteristic of an individual which is causally related to effective or superior performance in a job'. Competencies can be motives, traits, self-concepts, attitudes or values, content knowledge or cognitive or behavioural skills. At the level of the organization, a process of isolating and measuring so-called 'core competencies' is required. It is these core competencies that can then be used for selection, training and reward management purposes. A summary list for senior managers might include the following:

- analytical thinking;
- pattern recognition;
- strategic thinking;
- persuasion;

- use of influence strategies;
- personal impact;
- motivating.

These can be built into the appraisal system, and rewarded according to standards attained in each area.

Linking competencies to explicit forms of behaviour ensures that they are linked to the type of performance which contributes to organizational goals. Figure 4.6 provides an example in relation to behaviour towards customers.

Implementing skill-based and competency-based pay schemes requires a considerable investment in time and the establishment of procedures. Care must be taken to ensure that the cost of this investment and the imposition of overelaborate procedures do not outweigh the benefits of these schemes.

Performance management

Improving performance is the principal goal of most managers, and the reward system should contribute to this goal. Performance management is a term used to describe a process of ensuring that all employees participate in setting targets which contribute to the goals of the enterprise, are rewarded if they achieve these targets, and are provided with the training and resources needed to achieve their targets. In this way rewards and appraisal are linked into the total process of directing and managing the organization.

Well-developed performance management systems will usually incorporate the following items:

- A minimum statement, outlining the organization's values.
- A statement of the organization's objectives.
- Individual objectives are linked to the organization's objectives.
- Regular performance reviews throughout the year.
- Performance-related pay.
- Training and counselling.

An example of this system in practice, in this case from British Airways, is shown in Figure 4.7.

On the face of it, performance management appears to be the sensible way of managing any organization, and the wonder is that

This section explains what is meant by the term 'Key Result Area' and 'Specific Key Result' and helps you to set them.

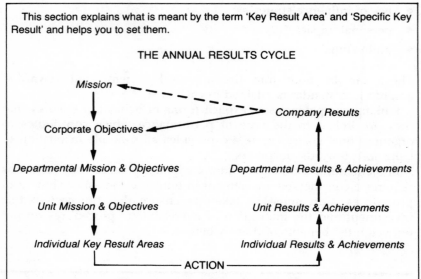

THE ANNUAL RESULTS CYCLE

The cycle links your effort to your unit results and ultimately to the company results. Note that the only way that results can be achieved at any level is through the individual – You!

- You have customers and stakeholders who expect something from you – every unit, every job has a purpose
- The broad purpose (mission) and success criteria can be described
- The key areas of activity, specific results and outputs which will achieve the purpose should be described and regularly reviewed with stakeholders and customers

WHAT ARE KEY RESULT AREAS?

Key Result Areas are critical spheres of work within which you will achieve the main results and outputs of your job – the Key Results.

They are not a list of duties in the job.

Each KRA is a heading or very brief description of a vital area of activity.

Figure 4.7 Performance management – an example from a typical company handbook, describing key result areas and the annual results cycle

any organization should choose not to operate in this way. However, the evidence is that perhaps only one-fifth of large organizations have as yet adopted a performance-management approach, and it is problematic whether all those who have adopted it have implemented it in full. Some of the practical problems have already been indicated, notably the tension between pay and training. Where performance management has been adopted, its success has been limited in those companies which have:

- adopted a reactive rather than proactive strategy;

- not sufficiently involved line management;
- created a climate of fear;
- overemphasized bottom-line results;
- introduced it simply as a performance-related pay scheme;
- developed too much red tape.

But when these mistakes have not been made, or have been rectified, it has generally succeeded.[12,13] It is not yet possible to demonstrate a long-term link between performance management and economic success, and time will tell. But it represents a far more sensible system of motivating and rewarding staff than the old-fashioned bureaucratic structures it is replacing.

References

1. Kanter, R. M. *et al.*, 'The quiet revolution in pay practices', *Personnel*, special issue, January 1987.
2. Herzberg, F., 'One more time: how do you motivate employees?', *Harvard Business Review*, January–February 1968, pp. 53–62.
3. Lawler, E. E. and Porter, L. W., 'Antecedent attitudes of effective managerial performance', *Organisational Behaviour and Human Performance*, **2**, 1967, pp. 122–42.
4. Locke, E. A. *et al.*, 'Goal setting and task performance, 1969–1980', *Psychological Bulletin*, **90**, 1981, pp. 125–51.
5. Drucker, P., *The Practical Practice of Management*, Mercury Books, London: William Heinemann, 1961, Ch. 11.
6. Murlis, H. and Fitt, D., 'Job evaluation in a changing world', *Personnel Management*, May 1991, pp. 39–43.
7. Cannell, M. and Long, P., 'What's changed about incentive pay?', *Personnel Management*, October 1991, pp. 58–63.
8. Fletcher, C. and Williams, R., *Performance Appraisal and Career Development*, London: Hutchinson, 1985.
9. Yeates, J. D., *Performance Appraisal: A guide for design and implementation*, Institute of Manpower Studies Report No. 188, 1990
10. Edward, E. and Lawler, M., 'Paying the person: a better approach to management?', *Human Resource Management Review*, **1**(2), 1991.
11. Incomes Data Services Ltd, *Skill-based Pay*, IDS study 500, February 1992.
12. Fletcher, C. and Williams, R., 'The route to performance management', *Personnel Management*, October 1992.
13. Incomes Data Services Ltd, *Performance Management*, IDS study 518, November 1992.

5

Change, quality and integration

The principal difference between managing today and managing twenty years ago lies in the greater pace of change which managers now have to cope with. Society, technology and markets are changing rapidly, and organizations need to keep up with these changes if they are to survive. Yet most people tend to be conservative by nature and are not comfortable with too great a rate of change. Managers not only have to cope with change themselves but also have to ensure that their staff adapt to new ways of working. In this chapter we examine four key elements in this process of adaptation and change which now lie at the heart of the successful management of people. These are culture, training, communications and continuous improvement. Managers are being expected to meet higher standards of quality than before and are being caught up in programmes for total quality and continuous improvement. Personnel management and training processes lie at the heart of these trends.

Culture

We are familiar with the idea that a nation or a society has a culture that distinguishes it from other nations and societies. Individuals and groups behave differently in different societies because the, largely unwritten, rules of behaviour are different. Organizations, particularly large organizations, can be viewed as societies in miniature, and possess their own cultures. Such cultures, in turn, are unique and bring powerful pressures to bear on individuals and groups to conform to expected patterns of behaviour. The culture of an organization cannot be separated from the culture of the society within which it is located, and to understand and possibly try to change the culture prevailing within an organization we also have to take into account the relevant societal culture.

In recent years major organizations in Western industrialized nations have begun to take the subject of culture and change seriously. Previously it was regarded as a soft topic of no great significance to managers who were expected to focus on 'hard' topics like money and systems. It has come as something of a shock to many Western managers to find that the Japanese and other countries of the Pacific rim take culture very seriously, and that this contributes to their productivity and economic success.

In actual fact a significant proportion of Western organizations have also taken culture seriously for many years, although they may have used other names to describe it. This fact was brought out in a book published in 1982 in the United States, and published subsequently in many other countries. This book has probably done more than any other publication to place culture firmly on the agenda of boards of directors in Britain and elsewhere. It was written by two management consultants, Tom Peters and Robert Waterman, and called *In Search of Excellence*.[1] Written in response to the threat of Japanese economic competition, it reported on the findings of a study of so-called 'excellent' American companies that, by various commercial yardsticks, were considered to be outstandingly successful. The aim was to find whether there existed any common denominators for success. Although some of the organizations featured in their study were unable to maintain the excellence of their reputation in later years, the majority are still highly respected institutions.

Peters and Waterman claimed to have uncovered eight attributes that distinguished excellent and innovative companies. These eight attributes have now entered the everyday speech of managers everywhere; they are:

- a bias for action;
- close to the customer;
- autonomy and entrepreneurship;
- productivity through people;
- hands on, value driven;

- stick to the knitting;
- simple form, lean staff;
- simultaneous loose–tight properties.

As Peters and Waterman commented in their book, many of these were not startling, and indeed could be recognized as 'motherhoods'. The point was, however, that excellent companies really put these precepts into practice. (For a fuller explanation of these attributes see Chapter 1 of *In Search of Excellence*.)

The fifth attribute, 'Hands on, value driven', is particularly relevant to this chapter, because it concerns culture. Peters and Waterman said of this fifth attribute, 'let us suppose that we are asked for one all-purpose bit of advice for management, one truth that we were able to distil from the excellent companies research. We might be tempted to reply "Figure out your value system. Decide what your company stands for." We are struck by the explicit attention they pay to values, and by the way in which they their leaders have created exciting environments through personal attention persistence, and direct intervention far down the line.'[2]

Peters and Waterman underline the significance of value systems in helping or hindering the achievement of excellence. Essential to success was that all staff, from top to bottom, should subscribe to a common set of values that influenced in a powerful way the working behaviour of employees in striving towards common organizational goals. This is illustrated in their so-called '7-S' model illustrated in Figure 5.1, where shared values lie at the heart of the diagram.

Earlier investigations had already pointed to differences in emphasis between American and Japanese companies.[3] In particular, it was considered that American managers had traditionally placed their emphasis on the 'hard' factors depicted in the top half of this diagram, namely strategy, structure and systems, and looked down on the 'soft' factors, namely skills, staff and style. In contrast to this, Japanese managers place great emphasis on the 'soft' factors. Peters and Waterman's findings indicated that all Western managers should take these soft factors seriously if they are to achieve excellence and to compete successfully with high-quality Japanese products.

A spate of further research studies and publications has followed on from Peters and Waterman's study, many of them focusing on culture and shared value systems. These have also tended to underline the contribution shared value systems make to organizational success.[4]

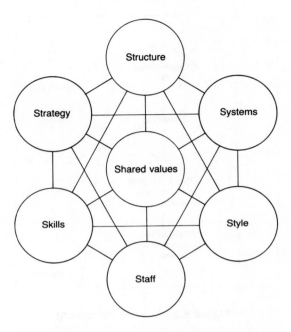

Figure 5.1 McKinsey 7-S framework

To help us to understand culture at societal level we can turn to the work of sociologists and anthropologists. A typical example is provided by the British sociologist Stephen Cotgrove, who sought to explain social systems and culture in terms of values, norms, knowledge and ideologies.[5] Values he saw as being concerned with 'ends', and norms as being concerned with 'means'. If this line of thinking is applied to organizations as being small-scale social systems, then the following questions can be asked about a particular organization:

- What are the prevailing values?
- What norms of behaviour, written or unwritten, influence behaviour?
- How well informed are employees on company matters?
- What ideologies about the company are prevalent?

If the aim is to change the culture of an organization as well as to understand it, then change will have to take place at all these levels.

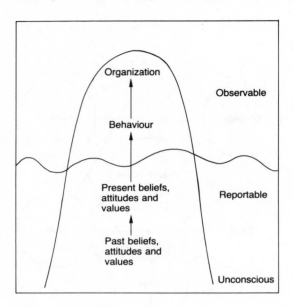

Figure 5.2   The cultural iceberg

Finding answers to these questions at more than a superficial level may not be easy. A useful analogy is provided by an iceberg. Only one-sixth of an iceberg is visible above the waterline. So it is with human behaviour in organizations. We can observe actions, but values are much harder to observe. Take, for example, Figure 5.2, values and attitudes are largely out of sight underneath the 'waterline'. However, we can use attitude and opinion surveys to indicate where values may lie. Thus organizations are turning increasingly to regular attitude surveys amongst employees to measure whether values are indeed changing. There is an alternative approach to culture and behaviour, which might be termed a 'behaviourist' view, and which has an appeal for practical managers. This view sidesteps any detailed investigation of values as a waste of time and attempts to tackle behaviour directly by the use of rewards and punishments. Although there is little doubt that behaviour can, in the short term, be changed in this manner, this approach can fail to win hearts and minds, and unless hearts and minds are won over employees will not be committed to change in the manner now required in today's highly competitive environment.

Two well-known definitions of organization culture illustrate alternative approaches:

- 'Corporate culture is the pattern of basic assumptions that a given group has invented, discovered or developed in learning to cope with its problems of external adaptation and internal integration' – Ed Schein, social psychologist.[6]
- 'The way we do things around here' – Marvin Bower, managing director of a firm of management consultants (quoted in Deal and Kennedy's book on corporate culture).[7]

So management may attempt to change 'the way things are done around here' by direct intervention, orders, rewards and personal example. Or they may attempt to alter patterns of basic assumptions by, for example, informing, educating and advising. Or they may try to do both. We shall return to this theme after we have examined a popular typology of organization culture developed by a well-respected American organization development expert, Roger Harrison.

Roger Harrison described four types of organization culture that prevail in different situations:[8]

- role culture;
- power culture;
- achievement culture;
- support culture.

A role culture emphasizes order stability and control, and is based on a quest for security. Typical of a role culture might be an old-fashioned public-sector bureaucracy. A power culture emphasizes strength, decisiveness and determination, and is based on a quest for security. Power cultures are found in some large, private-sector organizations, where a handful of senior executives exert a large amount of power in an autocratic manner, and in privately owned, smaller organizations, where the controlling family may wield considerable power. Achievement cultures emphasize success, growth and distinction, and are based on self-expression. They may be found in some modern progressive organizations that encourage autonomy and self-expression. Support cultures are based on mutual service, integration and values, and are based on a sense of community.

Charles Handy has adapted this approach in Britain and has come

Culture	Diagrammatic representation	Structure
Power or club		Web
Role	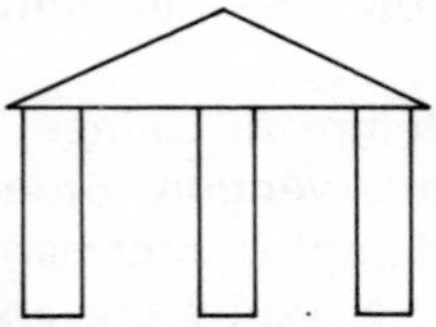	Greek temple
Task	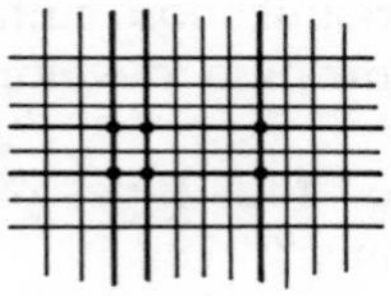	Net
Person or existential		Cluster

Source: Adapted from Handy, C.B., *Understanding Organizations*, London: Penguin, 1976.

Figure 5.3   Charles Handy's four cultures

up with four types of organization culture, which correspond with conceptual 'maps' of organization structures. These are power cultures and role cultures (similar to Harrison's categories), task cultures and person cultures. Task cultures place emphasis on the successful achievement of tasks, and person cultures refer to organizations designed to create space for individuals to operate in and be creative. These are shown in Figure 5.3.

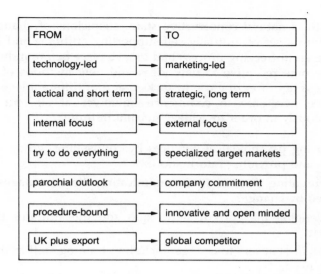

Figure 5.4 Changing the company culture at ICL

Both these approaches link the predominant value system, or culture, to the design of the organization, suggesting a match between structure and culture. This provides a useful reminder that if an organization makes major changes to its structure it will need to promote a new and more congruent culture, and vice versa.

Changing the culture of an organization is difficult, and requires time, resources, patience and relevant skills and leadership. Yet it is something organizations are having to tackle in order to respond to changes in their markets and economic, social and political environments. An example of this is provided by the company ICL, already featured in Chapter 2 as an organization that had to go through a major change programme in order to survive in the face of fierce competition. At the heart of this change programme was a strategic initiative to change the culture of the company (Figure 5.4). Although launched in the 1980s and reckoned by many to have been a success, ICL consider that the process of culture is still ongoing.

Culture change requires a strategy that takes in the whole organization. Change at a more modest level has been the focus of organization design (OD) specialists for the past thirty years and more. One of the earliest models for introducing successful change into a department, or a part of the organization, and still popular today is provided by Kurt Lewin.[9] Lewin argues that it was not feasible to expect people to change while they were still 'cold', i.e.

were in their natural conservative state, suspicious of change and 'frozen' into a set of mutually self-supporting attitudes and habits. Therefore an unfreezing process had to take place before individuals would become receptive to new ideas and new methods of work. The process of unfreezing can be tackled at four different levels, and it may be necessary to commence initiatives at all four levels simultaneously in order to achieve maximum input:

1. Reducing psychological defences by counselling, group discussions and providing information.
2. Accentuating benefits by communicating the advantages to be gained by change.
3. Challenging the current status quo and the attitudes that go with it.
4. Removing barriers to change, including training staff in the new skills needed.

Following on from the 'unfreezing' process, changes can be implemented involving individuals, jobs, technology and structures. The final phase is one of 'refreezing' when individuals are convinced of the benefits of the changes and the new pattern becomes integrated into work-group norms. This three-stage model is depicted in Figure 5.5.

To Lewin we also owe the useful model of change known as the 'force field' model. This works on the assumption that at any given time there is likely to be a state of equilibrium between the forces for change and the forces against change. If we want to bring about change, we must disturb this equilibrium in a planned manner by strengthening appropriate forces for change or weakening the forces inhibiting change, or both. It is, of course, first necessary within an organization to identify the respective forces for and against change.

An example of this is provided in Figure 5.6. This model was developed during a project investigating culture change in a sample of British organizations, sponsored by the Institute of Personnel Management.[10] This project focused on methods of changing culture that were linked to activities associated with personnel and training

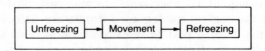

Figure 5.5 Lewin's change model

Source: Williams, A., Dobson, R. and Walters, M., *Changing Culture*, London: Institute of Personnel Management, 1989, p. 56.

Figure 5.6 Factors influencing the rate of change of organizational culture

departments. Traditionally, personnel departments have been perceived as forces for conservatism and status quo, bastions of bureaucratic rules and regulations. Modern human resource management departments have attempted to break this mould, and to be forces for progressive change, working closely with line managers. Normal personnel processes and services can, in fact, be used in a powerful fashion to reinforce change, as shown in case-study organizations described in this book, for example:

1. *Recruitment and selection.* Recruitment and selection can bring in new people with new ideas. Selection, in turn, can be carried out in a more scientific fashion.
2. *Pay systems.* New ways of rewarding employees linking pay to performance and improving appraisal systems create very strong signals for change. Reinforcement is provided for behaving in accordance with the desired culture.
3. *Quality programmes.* Introducing total quality programmes frequently requires a major culture change as individuals take personal responsibility for quality.
4. *Redundancy.* Redundancy programmes provide a strong negative signal that the organization is serious about changing working practices.
5. *Management development programmes.* These can develop new ways of thinking and new competencies amongst managers.
6. *Customer awareness programmes.* These programmes should help to change attitudes and behaviour towards customers and clients.
7. *Communications.* A range of communication channels can be utilized in support of culture change (a method explored later in this chapter).

Case studies of successful culture-change programmes in British organizations possess a number of common features. These features are largely in line with common sense as well as the points already made in this chapter. To be successful, programmes need, in the first place, to be strategic in their scope. That is to say, they must encompass the whole organization and be carefully planned and integrated with the mission and objectives of the organization. Secondly, they require an adequate investment of resources to fund the various initiatives required. Thirdly, they require leadership of a high order from the top. Fourthly, they require acceptance of the need for change at all levels in the organization. Unfortunately, this tends to come about in British organizations only when there is a crisis of major proportions that threatens the future of the organization and the employment prospects of all employees. Fifthly, there must be a recognition that culture change takes time, usually extending to several years. And finally, culture change must encompass all levels, including operatives and clerical employees. Too many culture-change programmes have failed because it is assumed that it is sufficient to get senior and middle management to subscribe to the new ways of doing things, when what is needed is a 'hearts and minds' campaign that is effective throughout the organization.

Communications

Successful change and integration require good communication. This fact has been recognized by management ever since management came into existence. And yet the first complaint one hears in most organizations is that communications are poor.

To be effective in communication, the organization must satisfy at least three criteria – quantity, quality and credibility. There must be sufficient information concerning what is happening and what is planned to happen. This information must be communicated in a clear manner using the appropriate media and with feedback channels. And the information must be trusted, which means in turn that the information source must be trusted, if it is to be believed. Traditionally, management has focused on the first of these, sometimes paying attention to the second, and all too frequently neglecting the third.

A surplus of information simply leads to information 'overload' and an excessive use of paper or electronic mail. Quality is achieved by forethought, training communication skills and use of appropriate organization structures and culture. Taking the last point first, a major weakness of traditional bureaucratic hierarchical structures is that communications are treated as a one-way process, with top management attempting to send information 'down the line' in the expectation that it will pass through successive layers in the structure until it reaches the worker or the shop floor. Some of the negative features associated with this type of structure were explored in Chapter 2. Most of us are painfully aware that information becomes distorted as it gets passed on, and is liable to misinterpretation. Information does not 'travel up the line' from bottom to top of the organization, and senior management remains in blissful ignorance about the attitudes and intentions of employees until it is too late. Furthermore, loyalty in this type of organization is primarily to one's own department, and therefore information is used as a tool in power struggles between different departments, frequently being withheld when it should be passed on, to the detriment of the organization as a whole. In more modern 'organic' types of organization structure, information flows more freely as decision-making is delegated and project management prevails.

The use of channels of information has greatly improved in recent years. Company newsletters are less likely to carry boring pictures of the chief executive on the front cover, and more likely to feature items of real interest to employees. The quality of written memoranda, however, has not improved in many cases, reflecting as it does the poor quality of education and training of staff. Skills in desktop publishing are regrettably no substitute for a good grasp of English grammar and a clear and concise style of writing. Senior management today makes better use of direct communication to employees on important issues, and there is therefore less need for employees to go to their trade-union representatives to find out what is actually happening. Audio-visual communications, including the use of closed-circuit television and specially prepared television-style briefings, are used more frequently in organizations with a well-thought-out policy on communications.

So-called 'briefing groups' have assisted greatly with communications, when they have been operated properly. These require that supervisors should be briefed regularly, possibly weekly, on company matters, and should, in turn, brief their own working groups. To be successful this does require at the very least that supervisors are trained in the appropriate skills, that they are provided with useful and up-to-date information, and are used as upward channels of information providing feedback from the shop floor to management.

For information to be credible it must be believed and the sources of information must be trusted. In too many organizations the unofficial 'grapevine' of information is believed in preference to management pronouncements. A famous writer on organizations once said, 'Try honesty, it is the best policy'.[11] Employees soon learn whether they can trust official sources of information. It is particularly important when major changes are planned that organizations communicate accurately and in advance in a well-thought-out manner if they are to carry the staff with them in implementing the changes. This important topic of communications is examined further in Chapter 7 in the context of employee participation and employee relations.

Total-quality management and continuous improvement

Total-quality management (TQM) entered the vocabulary of management some years ago and has had an impact on personnel management and industrial relations policies ever since. In true British style, however, some organizations have rushed into TQM as the flavour of the month, and then retired hurt when it has not proved to be the 'quick fix' they were looking for in order to solve their basic managerial deficiencies. This is unfortunate because the fundamental concepts of TQM are very sound and relevant to modern organizations. Private-sector organizations who do not take quality seriously will soon become uncompetitive, while public-sector organizations will, likewise, earn a reputation for second-rate service.

Most people are aware that TQM emanates from Japan, where it is taken very seriously, especially in manufacturing. Some are also aware that the process actually originated in the United States, and was passed on to the Japanese during the post-war era of American support for Japanese rehabilitation. The American most closely associated with this was Edward Deming. Japanese manufacturing took it seriously, American manufacturing did not. America and, indeed, all Western industrial nations now have to take it seriously, confronted with the threat of import penetration by Japanese quality products. Although it is true to say that it has been largely associated with engineering and production management, with an emphasis on 'zero defects', TQM rests on a policy of 'productivity through people', adoption of an appropriate organizational culture and a major investment in training, which is relevant to all types of organization.

Different experts on TQM emphasize different aspects of the process. Crosby is associated with the slogans 'zero defects' and 'right first time', Deming with 'plan do check action', and Juran with 'fitness for use' and 'quality is a mission for satisfying customer expectations through continued improvement in all areas of activity'. The British Quality Association has put forward three alternative definitions of TQM. The first focuses on the so-called 'soft' qualitative characteristics, such as customer orientation, culture of excellence, removal of performance barriers, teamwork, training, employee participation and competition edge. The second places emphasis on 'harder' aspects, including production techniques such as systematic measurement and control of work, setting standards of performance and statistical procedures to assess quality. The third is a mixture of 'hard' and 'soft', comprising the three features of an obsession with quality, the need for a scientific approach and the view that all employees are part of the one team.[12] An experienced senior British consultant's view[13] is that total quality:

- is a process, not just a system – it requires change to organization culture;
- takes time and consumes effort and energy;
- needs commitment to an attitude and behaviour change on the part of every employee;
- needs to be tailored to each organization;
- is about customers – internal as well as external;
- is focused on continuous improvement.

An example of its adoption as a company philosophy and set of principles is provided by Scottish Steel, as follows.

Approach	Management led
Scope	Company-wide
Theme	Everyone responsible
Style	Prevention not detection
Standard	Right first time
Measure	Costs of quality

The emphasis on customers existing both inside as well as outside the organization has major implications for personnel and industrial relations departments as well as for other internal service departments. For a start, it means defining measures of quality, and ascertaining from internal customers whether a quality service is being provided to their satisfaction.

A recent investigation sponsored by the Institute of Personnel Management into the involvement of personnel departments in the implementation of quality management, uncovered four useful roles: change agent, hidden persuader, internal contractor and facilitator. The change-agent role involves a high-level contribution which is very visible to others in the organization. The second role, of hidden persuader, means operating at a strategic level with the chief executive, providing advice and assistance but in a manner that is not particularly visible to other departments. Additionally, as an internal contractor the department tends to operate at a functional or operational level, providing a service to other departments. In a facilitator role the department again works at operational level, providing hands-on support for line managers facilitating the whole process of introducing quality. The report on this investigation suggests that the following types of activity by the personnel department are particularly useful:[14]

- Training middle managers and supervisors in how to develop the quality process with their staff.
- Identifying the conditions necessary for the successful use of quality tools and techniques.
- Training/coaching facilitators, mentors and team members in interpersonal skills and in how to manage the quality process.
- Designing communication events and vehicles to publicize the launch of TQM.
- Consulting with employees and trade-union representatives about the introduction and development of quality management.
- Assisting the board to develop mission statements and prepare quality objectives for dissemination to staff and customers.

The case study on Rank Xerox provided at the end of this chapter illustrates many of the key points concerning quality and continuous improvement outlined above.

Training for change

Training is an integral part of personnel management. Training provides a process by which organizations can improve the levels of knowledge and skills of their employees to the point where they are able to achieve high productivity, quality of output and lower cost. This helps them to achieve competitive advantage and to provide an excellent service.

Training is a major area of activity and requires more than a

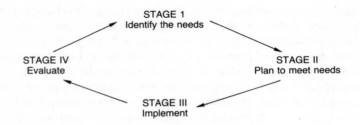

Figure 5.7   The systematic training cycle

section in a chapter to do it full justice. But training has also been affected by the same changes influencing other managers and employees. New approaches to training are emerging which in turn facilitate the processes of change. This is the 'essence' of training today, and a brief description is therefore appropriate in a book examining the 'essence' of personnel management.

The 1960s and 1970s witnessed something of a revolution in training in this country. Under the influence of training boards and fresh thinking about the training process from occupational psychologists, work-study engineers and trainers, great strides were made in developing training as a systematic process. An emphasis was laid on so-called 'terminal behaviour', this being a tight specification of the behavioural skills that a training programme should aim to achieve. Understandably, systematic training laid an emphasis on 'off the job' training, which was contrasted with the *laissez-faire* approach then so prevalent in British industry, typified in the phrase 'sitting by Nellie'. This systematic approach is illustrated in Figure 5.7.

Typically this approach required training objectives which were: 'clear and specific details, preferably formalised as a written statement and spelt out in precise behavioural, observable and measurable actions described by an action verb'.[15] Training was defined as 'the systematic development of the attitude/knowledge/skill behaviour pattern required by an individual in order to perform adequately a given task or job'.[16] Training procedures were recommended which were relevant to different levels within the hierarchy of the organization – typically for operatives, skilled craftsmen, clerical staff, supervisors and managers.

Today the emphasis has changed to a more holistic approach, treating the organization as a whole, and with a recognition that training can no longer assume a fairly static environment in which skills can be tightly specified. Skills have to be continuously updated as change occurs. It would be wrong, of course, to discard the lessons learnt from systematic training, and these can be integrated into flexible training.

The unfortunate reality in Britain is that a majority of organizations are reluctant to invest in training their employees. The customary reasons given for this are that training cannot demonstrate a financial 'pay-off' in the short term, and that any investment in training is likely to be lost when employees leave to join other organizations. Cumulatively, this creates a national profile of inadequate training which leaves us at a disadvantage compared with other countries, such as Germany and Japan, where employers do invest heavily in training, to their mutual advantage.

However, the pay-off from good training is measurable. Improvements in performance by operators under training has been well documented for many years. Today, training goes hand in hand with changes in work organization and new technology and progressive organizations, and measurement therefore has to relate to improvements resulting from the total process. A good example is provided by the Michelin tyre factory at Burnley in Lancashire, winners of *The Times* Award in the 1992 National Training Awards. Michelin state that they see training as being aimed at achieving quality, resulting in a people-development initiative, which has led to improvement in the factory's performance. 'Right first time levels, an important measure of factory performance, have steadily increased. Work-in-progress levels are now down by more than 73 per cent. Most important, at a time when reduced output had to be introduced, process and material costs have not been adversely affected. Flexibility and teamworking have undoubtedly paid off.'[17]

Flexibility and teamworking are key features of successful organization change. Teamworking requires training of the team as a whole as well as multiskilling members of the team so that they can do different jobs within the team, and of course training the team leader in leadership skills. Successful factories, such as the Nissan plant in the north-east of England, are based on the development of effective teams, with considerable authority delegated to team leaders. For each skill Nissan identifies a level of competence. Employees are encouraged to upgrade their skills continuously, progressing from the competence level 'Can do with reference to standard operation sheet', to the stage where they can not only perform all the standard operations but can train others (Figure 5.8).

The issue of competence was examined in Chapter 3 in the context of reward management. Its use in training has spread from its application within management development to all other areas of

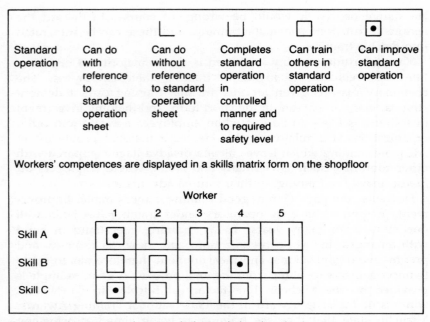

Each level of competence has a particular symbol assigned to it

Figure 5.8   The Nissan ILU progressive training system

training. The appeal to use the term 'competence' in preference to 'knowledge and skills' lies in the implied promise that competence will lead to higher output and a better performance, whereas knowledge and skills may not. It will be interesting to see whether this is in fact substantiated by research in due time. The government set a deadline that standards of competence should have been set for every industry in this country by the end of 1992, and this target has largely been reached. The government's Training Agency defines competence as '. . . the ability to perform the activities within an occupation or function to the standards expected in employment. Competence is a wide concept which embodies the ability to transfer skills and knowledge to new situations within the occupational area. It encompasses organisation and planning work, innovation and coping with non-routine activities. It includes those qualities of personal effectiveness that are required in the workplace to deal with co-workers, managers and customers.'[18]

The National Council for Vocational Qualifications (NCVQ) was established by the government in 1986 and was made responsible for ensuring that all industries set standards of competence. This task is being carried out by so-called Industry Lead Bodies. There are already indications that what started out as a good idea is being turned, British fashion, into a bureaucratic structure involving form-filling and red tape. Although centralized bodies can be of assistance provided they remember that they exist to provide a service and not to impose constraints, the primary focus in developing competencies should be within organizations. It is in the self-interest of organizations to train effectively and to develop their own standards of competence.

A supporting initiative from the central government has been the Investors in People programme, whereby companies can claim recognition for the training they are doing.[19] Companies have to satisfy a number of criteria, such as having a written plan showing how training relates to business goals and targets, clearly identified resources for training, evidence of training of new recruits as well as continuous development of all employees. Mechanisms have been set up on a regional basis to provide support for Investors in People programmes as well as promoting training generally in partnership with local employers. At least two-thirds of these TEC (Training Enterprise Councils) boards must consist of private-sector employers. Regrettably, no places are allocated to personnel and training managers who possess the relevant professional skills.

Perhaps the most exciting idea in training in recent years has been the so-called 'learning organization'. This is based on the organization being treated as a system (a concept familiar in so-called 'systems theory') that needs to respond to its environment in order to survive and prosper. In turn, this view requires that the organization develop a capability for responding to changes in its environment, which ensures that continuous internal transformation takes place. A learning organization has been defined as 'an organization which facilitates the learning of all its members and continuously transforms itself'.[20] This is not the same thing as a company that does a lot of training! Training is obviously a key feature, but training is subsidiary to the general aim of creating a culture of continuous learning in which all employees are involved. Human resource development is then integrated into the corporate strategy of the enterprise.

Peter Senge described the managerial qualities of a learning organization in terms of five disciplines.[21] These consist of a holistic approach to problem-solving, using 'soft' systems to define complex and interrelated problems in order to understand them fully; personal qualities of objectivity, focused energies and patience; shared mental models of the company; a shared vision of the future;

and collective or team learning. (For a good case-study example of these principles being put into practice see the article by David Beard 'Learning to change organisations' in *Personnel Management,* January 1993.)

Rank Xerox UK Ltd – a case study in integration, change and quality

Xerox is a multinational organization employing some 100 000 staff world-wide. The parent company is based in the United States and is responsible for all financial services, for the development and manufacture of most products and for the marketing and servicing of products in the USA. Rank Xerox is a joint venture between Xerox and the Rank Organization and is responsible for the marketing and servicing of Xerox products in Europe, Australia, New Zealand, Africa and the Middle East. Rank Xerox UK Ltd is responsible for the marketing and servicing of products in the UK.

Xerox introduced the first paper copier in 1959. For twenty years Rank Xerox dominated the photocopier market until the Japanese entered the market in the late 1970s. Profits began to tumble for Rank Xerox, and they were threatened with extinction. There was a fat middle-management structure, responsibilities were duplicated and communications were poor. The organization had become complacent. By the early 1980s Xerox was in a poor financial position.

The road to salvation was to be via a new philosophy of quality, competitive benchmarking, a new organizational culture and a new structure.

Fuji Xerox is a joint venture company in Japan. In 1976 Fuji Xerox launched a total-quality management programme that culminated in 1980 in their winning Japan's Deming prize for quality. This was to form the basis for Xerox's world-wide total-quality management programme. Their new philosophy which launched their climb back to success was stated in the following terms: 'Xerox is a quality company. Quality is the basic business principle for Xerox. Quality means providing our external and internal customers with innovative products and services that fully satisfy their requirements. Quality improvement is the job of every employee.'

Quality offices were established at Xerox headquarters and around the world. A detailed strategy and plan was put together. The theme 'Leadership through Quality' was adopted. Company literature describes this as first a goal, second a strategy and third a process: 'It is a goal because we have to attain it. It is a strategy because we will achieve a competitive edge and attain leadership in our chosen business through continuous pursuit of quality improvements. It is a process because in Xerox quality is the fundamental business principle upon which our management and work processes will be based.'

At the same time Xerox instituted a process called 'competitive benchmarking'. This means comparing yourself with, and learning from, others who have achieved high standards of excellence. It is an analytical process for measuring your operations against others already considered 'best in class', which allows the development and implementation of specifications to close the gap between you and your peers. One study found, for example, that Xerox's unit manufacturing cost was equal to the Japanese selling price in the United States – and the Japanese were still making a profit! Benchmarking revealed a need for a year-on-year growth rate of 18 per cent to catch up with Japan in a five-year period. It also revealed that it took Xerox twice as long to bring new products to market as the Japanese, and their defective parts greatly exceeded those found in Japanese products.

The organizational structure was changed from a classical 'command and control' organization with discreet functions such as sales, marketing, manufacture and finance organized on a formal hierarchical basis, to a cross-functional participative organization where team orientation and self-managed work groups became commonplace. To enable and facilitate this change, the role of the manager had to move from one of director and inspector of results to that of coach, facilitator and inspector of the process. The company priorities were restated as:

1. customer satisfaction;
2. employee satisfaction;
3. return on assets;
4. market share.

The management *raison d'être* was now one of supporting the front-line employees in providing customer satisfaction. This is shown in Figure 5.9, in which the traditional organization structure has been inverted.

The orientation was thus changed from one of internal process management to one of ensuring all processes were aligned with customer requirements. In consequence, the culture began to change. An empowerment strategy devolved responsibility and accountability to the employees closest to the customer. Layers of management were reduced. Statistical analysis, as recommended by TQM gurus such as Deming, Juran and Crosby, was introduced. Management processes were made cross-functional. Thus the management of sales, service and administration meet together to review their common goals and analyze issues which may be functional by nature but have an impact on the process of serving customers in the most effective way.

Four mechanisms have been used to reinforce the culture-change process:

1. *Recognition and rewards*. Rewards have been linked to 'quality' behaviour.

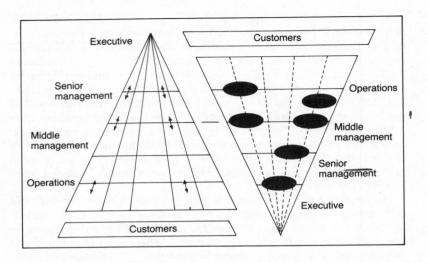

Source: Walker, R., 'Ranx Xerox – management revolution', *Long Range Planning*, **25**(1), 1992, p. 14.

Figure 5.9 Changing the organization structure and philosophy at Xerox

2. *Training*. Training has been provided in quality techniques such as statistical analysis and problem solving.
3. *Communications*. Journals, videos and meetings have been used to communicate company objectives.
4. *Leadership and management example*.

Today, in the view of senior management, they have succeeded in changing management philosophy, and the organization and value systems are changing fast in the right direction. Xerox has moved from being a copier company to being an information systems company. Return on investment and market share has improved. Xerox has come back from the brink and is now capable of meeting the challenge of any competition.

Sources of information for case study

Blackmore, P., Presentation at IPM Annual Conference, October 1990.
Walker, R., 'Rank Xerox – management revolution', *Long Range Planning*, **25**(1), 1992, pp. 9–21.
Williams, A., Dobson, P. and Walters, M., *Changing Culture: New organisational approaches*, Institute of Personnel Management, 1987.

References

1. Peters, T. J. and Waterman, R. H. Jnr, *In Search of Excellence*, New York: Harper & Row, 1982.
2. *ibid.*, p. 279.
3. Pascale, R. T. and Athos, A. G., *The Art of Japanese Management*, London: Simon & Schuster, 1981.
4. Deal, T. E. and Kennedy, A. *Corporate Cultures, the Rites and Rituals of Corporate Life*, Reading, MA: Addison-Wesley, 1982.
5. Cotgrove, S., *The Science of Society* (4th edn), London: George Allen and Unwin, 1978.
6. Schein, E., *Organisational Culture and Leadership*, San Francisco: Jossey Bass, 1985, p. 25.
7. Deal and Kennedy, *Corporate Life*, p. 4.
8. Harrison, R., 'Organisation culture', extract from talk to AMED Conference, *Association for Management Education and Development News*, May 1990.
9. Lewin, K., '*Field Theory in Social Science*', New York: Harper & Row, 1951.
10. Williams, A., Dobson, R. and Walters, M., *Changing Culture*, Institute of Personnel Management, 1989.
11. Townsend, R., *Up the Organisation*, London: Michael Joseph, 1970.
12. Wilkinson, A., Marchington, M. and Goodman, J., 'Total quality management and employee involvement', *Human Resource Management Journal*, 2(4), Summer 1992.
13. Wibberley, M., 'The road to total quality', paper presented to Institute of Personnel Management Annual Conference, 1989.
14. Marchington, M., Wilkinson, A. and Dale, B., 'Case study reports on quality', in *Quality, People Management Matters*, Institute of Personnel Management, 1993.
15. Livy, B., *Corporate Personnel Management*, London: Pitman, 1988, p. 143.
16. Baron, B., 'Systematic training', in *Managing Human Resources*, ed. Cowling, A. G. and Mailer, C., London: Edward Arnold, 1981.
17. Harris, D., 'Michelin shows training is the road to success', *The Times*, 12 May 1993.
18. Training Agency 'Development of assessable standards for national certification', Guidance Note 2, Employment Department, Moorfoot, 1989.
19. Critten, P., *Investing in People: Towards corporate capability*, Oxford: Butterworth-Heinemann, 1993.
20. Pedlar, M., Burgoyne, J. G. and Boydell, T. H., *The Learning Company: A strategy for sustainable development*, Maidenhead: McGraw-Hill, 1991.
21. Senge, P., *The Fifth Discipline: The art and practice of the learning organisation*, London: Random Century, 1990.

6

Occupational health and safety

Work-related illness and injuries have been a feature of employment since the beginning of industrialization. Such illness and injuries clearly have important physical, emotional and financial consequences for workers and their families. They can also have important legal and financial implications for employers.

This chapter begins with a brief discussion on the scale of work-related accidents and ill health and the costs of these for employers. The legal framework relating to occupational health and safety, and the way in which this is currently being affected by European Community (EC) activities, is then outlined. The concluding section goes on to examine the factors that affect the management of health and safety in organizations and the role of work-force involvement.

Accidents and ill health at work

Legal requirements relating to the reporting of certain types of accidents have existed since 1923. However, the nature of these reporting requirements and the types of activities covered by them have varied considerably over the years. The current requirements are contained in the *Reporting of Injuries, Diseases and Dangerous Occurrences Regulations* (RIDDOR) 1985.[1] In brief, these impose obligations on employers regarding the reporting of fatalities, 'major injuries', accidents causing workers to be absent from work for more than three days, and certain types of dangerous occurrences and occupational diseases.

In the year 1990–91 a total of 572 fatal accidents were reported under these requirements, 346 of which were suffered by employees, 87 by the self-employed and 139 to members of the public.[2] In addition, employees were reported to have suffered 19 896 major injuries and 160 811 over-three-day injuries.

Two important points must be borne in mind about these official statistics. First, and by definition, they exclude all accidents causing absences from work of three days or less. Secondly, their accuracy is crucially dependent on the extent to which employers comply with their reporting obligations. Recent data from the 1990 Labour Force Survey (LFS) indicate that as a result the official RIDDOR statistics considerably underestimate the scale of accidents occurring as a result of work-based activities. Thus analysis of these data suggests that the actual number of work-place accidents suffered by those in employment (employees and the self-employed) in 1990–91 totalled at least 1.4 million.[3] Of these, 620 000 were estimated to be legally reportable, suggesting that less than one-third of reportable non-fatal injuries at work are actually reported. More generally, the findings suggest that employed people took around 21.1 million days off work (including weekends) as a result of injuries incurred at work – considerably exceeding the number of days lost through strikes (see Chapter 9).

The LFS study also asked respondents about whether in the previous 12 months they had suffered any illness, disability or other physical problems which, in their view, had been caused or made worse by their work. The results obtained are shown in Figure 6.1. As can be seen, the number of cases reported exceed the number of accidents reported by respondents and in crude terms indicate that occupationally related ill health is an even more serious problem than that of work-place accidents.

Such statistics on accidents and ill health give only a very partial indication of the financial, physical and emotional suffering caused to workers and their families. Similarly, they give little insight into the financial consequences for employers. Recent research on the costs of accidents by the Accident Prevention Advisory Unit (APAU) of the Health and Safety Executive suggests, however, that these may be considerably larger than is frequently assumed by employers.[4]

The APAU study consisted of a series of five case studies carried out over periods ranging from 13 to 18 weeks on a construction site, a creamery, a transport company, an oil platform and a hospital.

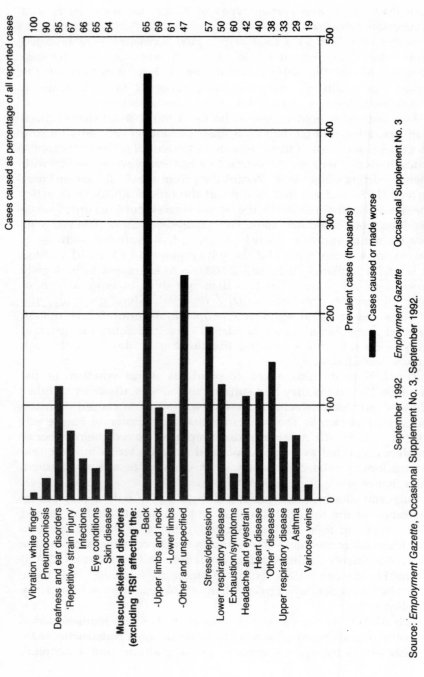

Figure 6.1 Estimated twelve-month prevalence of self-reported work-related illness, by disease category in England and Wales, spring 1990

Source: *Employment Gazette*, Occasional Supplement No. 3, September 1992.

The sites used for the studies employed between 70 and 800 people and each was considered to have average or better than average health and safety records.

During the studies, data were collected on over 6342 accidents, deemed to be economic to prevent, none of which involved fatalities, major injuries or large-scale loss through fire or explosion. Total losses incurred as a result of these accidents inevitably varied considerably, ranging from £940 000 on the oil platform to £49 928 in the transport company. In each case, however, the accidents were found to have important financial implications for the operations concerned. Thus, on an annual basis, it was calculated that they represented 8.5 per cent of the tender price of the construction organization, 1.4 per cent of the creamery's operating costs, 37 per cent of the transport company's profits, 14.2 per cent of the potential output of the oil platform and 5 per cent of the annual running costs of the hospital.

The legal framework

Common law

Workers who suffer injuries and ill health at work may be able to claim compensation from their employers.[5] Employer liability for such compensation can arise in two main ways: through actions for negligence and breach of statutory duty. Employers are legally obliged to possess insurance covering any compensation awards made against them in respect of employees.[6]

In common law employers have a duty of reasonable care towards their employees. If they breach this duty, that is fail to take reasonable care to prevent reasonably foreseeable dangers, then an action for negligence will succeed. Such liability, it should be noted, will also arise through the doctrine of vicarious liability. That is, where injuries or ill health result from the negligent actions of another employee committed during the course of their employment.

An action for breach of statutory duty allows a person to sue for damages where the employer's conduct resulting in the injury involved contravention of a duty imposed by statute. For a claim to be upheld, the plaintiff has first to establish that there was a breach of such a statutory duty and, secondly, show that this breach directly caused the injury in question. Since statutory duties often impose stricter and more precise duties than the common law, actions for breach of statutory duty are of greater practical importance than actions for negligence. It must, however, be noted that some statutory provisions, such as the general duties laid down under the Health and Safety at Work (HSW) Act (see below), specifically exclude their use as a basis for common law compensation claims.

Two main defences to common law actions for damages are available to employers: *violenti non fit injuria* and contributory negligence. The first of these defences, which will today only rarely succeed, is based on the principle that a plaintiff should not be able to recover damages if an injury arises from a risk that she or he agreed to accept. The second will succeed where it can be shown that the injured employee failed to take reasonable care for his or her own safety and hence contributed to the injuries. Where this is established, then the damages awarded will be reduced accordingly.

Statutory law

The history of protective health and safety legislation dates back to the Morals of Apprentices Act 1802, a statute enacted as a result of concern about the appalling working conditions of pauper children in cotton mills. The next 100 years saw the piecemeal extension of legislation to cover other types of worker, work-places and hazards. The result of this *ad hoc* process of legislative development meant that by the early 1970s a highly complex body of law had developed, consisting of nine main groups of statutes and nearly 500 supplementary statutory instruments. Notable among these statutes were the Factories Act 1961, the Mines and Quarries Act 1954 and the Offices, Shops and Railway Premises Act 1963.

In 1970 the Robens Committee was established to review the existing statutory framework for occupational health and safety, against a background of concern that the long-term trend towards improved standards of occupational health and safety had reached a plateau. In its subsequent report (1972) the Committee made three fundamental criticisms of the existing statutory framework.[7] First, it argued that there was 'too much law' and that this had the effect of generating apathy on the part of those in industry by encouraging them to think of 'safety and health at work as, in the first and most important instance, a matter of detailed rules imposed by external agencies'. Secondly, the Committee concluded that much of the present law was 'intrinsically unsatisfactory' in that it was largely unintelligible, failed to cover all work situations and was overly concerned with laying down prescriptive requirements in respect of physical hazards. Thirdly, it expressed concern with the existing 'fragmentation of administrative jurisdictions' between five government departments and seven separate inspectorates.

The Committee went on to put forward a range of reforms intended to achieve two main objectives: a unified and more integrated system which would improve the state's contribution to health and safety; and the creation of conditions that would lead to a more effective self-regulatory system. In particular, it recommended that the existing statutory measures should be replaced by a comprehensive and orderly set of revised provisions made under a new enabling Act. It was recommended that this Act include a clear statement of the basic principles of safety responsibility and be supported by regulations and non-statutory codes of practice. It should also extend to cover all employers and employees as well as the self-employed, whose acts and omissions could endanger other people or the general public. Finally, it recommended that the existing inspectorates should be amalgamated to form a unified service and that inspectors should be armed with new enforcement powers in the form of improvement and prohibition notices.

Although the subject of criticism from some quarters,[8] the Robens Committee's recommendations and analysis received widespread political support and formed the basis for what is now the centrepiece of Britain's statutory system for occupational health and safety – the Health and Safety at Work Act 1974. The Act, as recommended by Robens, is essentially an enabling statute which provides a framework within which the earlier provisions can be revised and replaced. Therefore, its implementation did not herald the large-scale repeal of existing statutes and statutory instruments. Instead, this earlier legislation remained in place pending its gradual replacement by new requirements under the 1974 Act.[9]

HSW Act administration and enforcement

The HSW Act established two new bodies to administer and enforce the statutory framework for occupational health and safety: the Health and Safety Commission (HSC) and the Health and Safety Executive (HSE). The HSC is a body corporate which must consist of a chairman and nine other members. It is structured on a tripartite basis. Thus three of its members are appointed after consultations with organizations representing employees, and three following consultations with organizations representing employers.

The HSC is charged with promoting the 'general purposes' of the Act. It also has a number of more specific duties. Perhaps the most important of these is to prepare regulations. In this connection it should be noted that the HSC is also empowered, for the purpose of providing practical guidance on the requirements imposed by statutory provisions, to issue codes of practice. Such codes do not in themselves have the force of law. However, where a person is alleged to have contravened a statutory requirement and it is shown that he or she has failed to observe a relevant code, then this will be taken as conclusive evidence of guilt, unless the defendant can satisfy the court that the relevant obligations have been complied with in some other way.

The HSE is in effect the operational arm of the HSC and its members are appointed by the HSC with the approval of the Secretary of State. On its creation on 1 January 1975 it became the employer of most of the inspectors who had been appointed under the earlier statutes. Inspections, however, also continue to be carried out by local authority inspectors in respect of a variety of 'non-industrial' activities.

HSE and local authority inspectors are given wide-ranging powers under the Act relating to such matters as: the right of entry to premises; the making of examinations and investigations; the taking of measurements, photographs and samples; the production and inspection of books and documents; the provision of facilities and assistance by employers; the questioning of people; and the seizing and rendering harmless of articles and substances. In addition, these inspectors can initiate prosecutions under the Act and issue improvement and prohibition notices.

An improvement notice can be served on an employer where an inspector is of the opinion that the person is contravening one or more relevant statutory provisions, or has done so in circumstances that make it likely that the contravention will continue or be repeated. Such a notice requires the person concerned to remedy the contravention or the matters occasioning it within a specified period. This period allowed must not be less than twenty-one days, the period within which appeals against notices may be lodged (see below).

Prohibition notices can be served by inspectors where the activities being, or about to be, carried out involve a risk of serious personal injury. The actual contravention of a relevant statutory provision is therefore not always necessary before a notice is served. A prohibition notice directs that the activities to which the notice relates should not be carried out unless the matters specified in it have been remedied. Such a notice may be issued with immediate effect.

A person on whom a notice is served has a right of appeal to an industrial tribunal within twenty-one days of the serving of a notice. In the case of an improvement notice, the effect of the appeal is to suspend its operation until the appeal is withdrawn or disposed of by a tribunal. A prohibition notice continues to operate, however, unless the tribunal chooses to order its suspension at the appeal or at a specially convened hearing. A tribunal is empowered to cancel or affirm a notice, either in its original form or with such modifications as are thought fit.

Prosecutions can be brought against any person or body corporate that contravenes any relevant statutory provisions. In addition, s.37(1) provides that where an offence committed by a body corporate is proved to have been committed with the consent or connivance of, or to have been attributable to any neglect on the part of, any director, manager, secretary or other similar officer, that person is also guilty of the offence. Some types of offence may only be tried summarily before a magistrates' court. Others may also be tried on indictment before a crown court. These latter offences cover such matters as a failure to comply with an improvement or prohibition notice and a failure to discharge any of the general duties laid down under the HSW Act and any health and safety regulations made under it.

A person convicted of an offence on summary conviction can be fined a maximum of £500 unless the offence consists of breaching of ss.2–6 of ther HSW Act, in which case the maximum rises to £20 000. This maximum also applies where a person has been found guilty of failing to comply with an enforcement notice. In addition, such a person can also be imprisoned for up to six months. Convictions on indictment, in contrast, can lead to the imposition of an unlimited fine and, in the case of certain offences (such as non-compliance with an enforcement notice), up to two years' imprisonment.

General duties

Sections 2–9 of the 1974 Act specify a number of general duties. These impose obligations on employers and employees as well as the self-employed, the controllers of premises, and the designers, suppliers, manufacturers and importers of articles and substances for use at work. Most of these duties are qualified by the words 'so far as is reasonably practicable'. This phrase is not defined in the Act, but judicial decisions in various civil cases indicate that it involves balancing the risk to health and safety against the cost and trouble associated with its control.[10] In other words, the qualification involves a form of cost–benefit analysis.

Sections 2 and 3 of the Act detail the main duties of employers under the Act. By virtue of s.2(1) all employers are required to ensure, so far as is reasonably practicable, the health, safety and welfare at work of their employees. A similar duty is imposed under s.3(1) in respect of non-employees who may be affected by the employer's activities. Subsection 2(2) goes on to detail a number of matters to which this overall duty of care extends. These cover such matters as the provision and maintenance of plant and systems of work; arrangements concerning the use, handling, storage and transport of articles and substances; the provision, instruction, training and supervision of employees; and the provision and maintenance of safe means of access to and egress from the work-place. Finally, s.2(3) requires employers with five or more employees to prepare and, as often as may be appropriate, revise a written statement of general policy with respect to the health and safety of their employees and the organization and arrangements in force for carrying out that policy.

These general duties, as indicated earlier, are additional to the duties laid down under any of the earlier statutory provisions that remain in force. They have also been supplemented, and in some cases extended, by subsequent obligations imposed under various sets of regulations made under the HSW Act itself. In fact, a large number of such regulations have been made. Indeed the pace of their introduction has increased recently as a result of directives emanating from the EC.

Involvement in issues relating to worker health and safety was envisaged from the outset in each of the three founding European treaties: the European Coal and Steel Treaty, the Treaty of Rome and the EURATOM Treaty. However, with the partial exception of the last of these, no specific legislation-making powers were provided. Consequently, European Commission proposals relating to health and safety matters, other than ionizing radiations, had to be progressed by means of unanimity under the more general decision-making powers provided by Article 100 of the Treaty of Rome: an article concerned with initiatives relating to the establishment and functioning of the common market.

This situation changed dramatically with the advent of the Single European Act (SEA) 1986. The SEA introduced a new Article 118A into the Treaty of Rome, which for the first time gave the EC direct authority to take legislative action in respect of health and safety matters and also provided for proposals in the area to be adopted by qualified majority voting. The introduction of this new Article has resulted in a dramatic increase in the scale of EC health and safety legislation, both in terms of the number of proposals put forward and the speed with which these have been adopted. Thus the period since the adoption in 1988 of the EC's third action programme on health and safety has seen more than twenty directives adopted under Article 118A.[11]

All of these directives require amendments to be made to UK law and, in a significant number of cases, the making of new sets of regulations. For example, regulatory packages on display-screen equipment, manual handling, personal protective equipment and the use of work equipment have been introduced.[12] All of these regulations have stemmed from directives adopted under the umbrella of the EC's framework directive, which essentially constitutes a European equivalent of the HSW Act.[13] It is, however, far more detailed than the Act in terms of the duties imposed on employers. As a result its adoption has resulted in the introduction of perhaps the most important regulations to be made under the 1974 Act, the Management of Health and Safety at Work (MHSW) Regulations 1992.[14] These Regulations, which also implement an EC directive on the protection of temporary workers, lay down important new duties regarding:

- the carrying out and recording of risk assessments;
- the making and giving effect to arrangements for the planning, organization, control, monitoring and review of protective and preventive measures;
- co-operation and co-ordination of measures with other employers sharing the same work-place;
- the appointment of 'competent persons' to assist employers in developing protective and preventive measures;
- the giving of various types of information to employees, non-employees, temporary workers, employment businesses and other employers;
- the provision of training to employees on employment and when risks change;
- the establishment of procedures for serious and imminent danger; and
- the provision of health surveillance.

Management of health and safety at work

Much research has been conducted by psychologists, sociologists and economists into the causes of work accidents. These have been grouped usefully under three headings: the individual who causes the accident, the risks inherent in the work itself and the work–social environment.[15]

In the past, considerable attention was paid to examining the role played by such matters as age, job experience and perception of risk in explaining accidents. More recently, however, attention has tended to focus more on the way in which accident rates are influenced by aspects of the working environment, such as working hours and shift patterns, workload, the nature and extent of management–worker communications, and the provision made for work-force involvement (see below). For example, several recent studies have examined whether trends in accident rates are influenced by variations in work intensity and, linked to this, shifts in the balance of power between employers and workers. These have provided some evidence that the worsening of accident rates in the first half of the 1980s was particularly concentrated in industries characterized by high increases in productivity, low wages, weak trade-union organization and a relatively high concentration of employment in small work-places.[16]

The reason for the well-established inverse relationship between accident rates and work-place size is the subject of some debate. One contributory factor, however, is likely to be the fewer resources, both physical and human, that such work-places devote to health and safety. This explanation therefore serves to raise the question more generally of the role that employer policies play in determining standards of work-place health and safety. Inevitably this is difficult to quantify in any precise way. Research conducted by the HSE (and others) and the results of recent public inquiries into disasters such as Piper Alpha, Clapham Junction, Zeebrugge and King's Cross do, however, indicate that they play a crucial role.[17]

An HSE analysis of over 1000 fatal accidents found that the vast majority could have been avoided through the taking of reasonably practical precautions, in other words by employers and employees fulfilling their statutory duties under the HSW Act.[18] Of particular note was the HSE's conclusion that management failures were the primary cause of more than 60 per cent of the accidents examined. Interestingly, 'software' failures, such as the provision of inadequate training and supervision, or the use of unsafe systems of work, were found to have been more frequent causes of accidents than 'hardware' ones.

The disaster reports referred to above tend to bear this last point out. That concerning the Clapham Junction accident provides a good illustration. The broad details of this accident are as follows. On the morning of Monday 12 December 1988 a commuter train from Basingstoke was approaching Clapham Junction station when it crossed a signal as it suddenly turned to red. The driver, in accordance with standard operating procedures, stopped the train and went to phone the signal box to report that he had crossed a signal at 'danger'.

In doing so the driver was confident that the signal would remain at red while his train remained on that portion of the track. Unfortunately, this confidence proved to be misplaced and the signal reverted to yellow. As a result another commuter train entered the same stretch of track and crashed into the back of the Basingstoke train. This collision in turn forced the second train to its offside, where it was struck by another coming in the opposite direction. Thirty-five people died and nearly 500 were injured, 69 of them seriously.

British Rail (BR) staff quickly identified the immediate cause of the accident. An extra wire was found to be connected to a fuse on the signal and to be making contact with a relay on the Clapham 'A' signal box. This wire caused the faulty signal to show yellow rather than red. The official inquiry found that the presence of the additional wire was the result of faulty rewiring work carried out on a Sunday two weekends previously. However, the chairman of the inquiry, while accepting that the technician in question carried a heavy burden of responsibility for the accident, went on to argue that this responsibility had to be shared with many others within BR management. For example, it was found that the technician had not been provided with much relevant training or a copy of the departmental instruction outlining the safety precautions that should be taken when carrying out rewiring work. Moreover, some of the errors committed by the technician had been a feature of his work since he joined BR in 1972. Apparently no supervisor had ever complained that he was working in an unsafe or improper way.

In fact the official inquiry report reveals a whole series of weaknesses in the way in which health and safety was managed within BR. These included: confusion among supervisory and managerial personnel about their role in checking rewiring work; excessive reliance on overtime working; inadequate systems for monitoring breakdowns in safety systems; and a procedure for appraising investment decisions which provided an 'organizational disincentive' to safety. The report went on to make no fewer than ninety-three recommendations aimed at securing higher levels of safety on the railways.

Findings such as these bear out much academic research on how health and safety is managed in many organizations. All too often it has been found that health and safety issues are not approached in a thorough and systematic way, and are accorded insufficient importance in organizational decision-making concerning the allocation of human and financial resources. This, in turn, is seen to reflect the fact that such issues are rarely paid enough attention by senior management, with the consequence that they are not adequately integrated into general line management. In other words, as one researcher has put it, health and safety is too too frequently treated as a 'side-car' issue rather than as an integral part of management systems of control and decision-making.[19]

Effective safety management

Based on case-study research in a number of industries, Dawson and her colleagues have developed a prescriptive model of the elements necessary for effective health and safety management.[20] They divide these into two categories: organizational 'capacity' and 'willingness' to act. The first of these is analyzed in terms of the technical control of hazards, the second in terms of motivation and commitment to the issue of health and safety.

The complete model is summarized in Figure 6.2. As can be seen, six processes are seen as central to the effective management of health and safety:

- hazard identification and assessment;
- prescription and implementation of control measures;
- maintenance, monitoring and adaption of control standards and procedures;
- demonstration of positive commitment, including the development of a clear and appropriate safety policy;
- definitions of individual responsibilities; and
- systems of individual accountability.

To assist them in carrying out these types of activity many organizations, although a small minority overall, employ safety specialists – often called safety officers or advisers. The role of such specialists varies, but typically involves some combination of the activities detailed in Table 6.1. In general, however, their role is usually advisory rather than executive: an approach endorsed by the

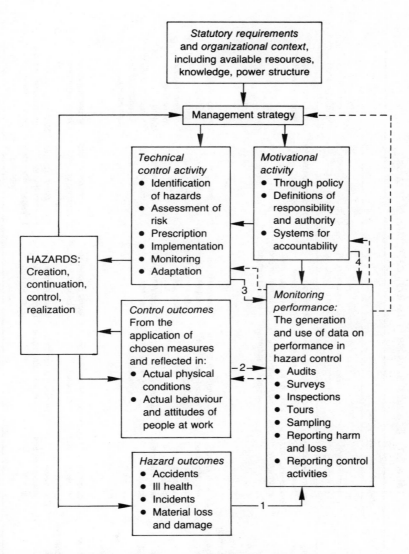

Source: Dawson *et al.*, 'Safety at work: the limits of self-regulation', Cambridge:
Cambridge University Press, 1988.

Figure 6.2 Model of the health and safety management process

Table 6.1   Specialist activities in the technical control of hazards

Safety specialists' activities	Stage of technical control				
	1. Identification of hazards	2. Assessment of risk	3. Development of controls	4. Implementation of controls	5. Longer-term monitoring and adaptation
A Processing information	Keeping accident statistics Processing hazard information	Calculating accident frequencies, etc. Processing information on hygiene standards	Processing equipment manufacturers' information and lists of products, etc.	Processing orders for safety equipment	Comparing accident statistics over time
B Giving advice/ problem-solving					
B1 Passive adviser	Looking at work operations, on request Investigating complaints	Answering questions about severity of hazards	Commenting on available controls which have been suggested	Commenting on effectiveness on request	Investigating accidents Inspecting Providing feedback on request
B2 Active adviser	Taking initiative in looking for hazards	Lobbying for appropriate standards, control limits	Recommending controls	Identifying shortfalls and improvements	Making recommendations for update/review of systems
C Taking direct executive action					
C1 Jointly with line management	Doing joint inspections and audits	Jointly deciding on standards	Jointly drawing up codes of practice	Joint supervision and approval or disapproval to jobs	Partipating in reviews of arrangements
C2 Alone	Doing own inspections and audits	Deciding unilaterally what is safe/unsafe	Issuing instructions Specifying controls to be followed	Supervising job Exercising veto Physically stopping people working	Modifying procedures, etc. on own initiative

Source: Dawson et al., 'Safety at work: the limits of self-regulation', Cambridge: Cambridge University Press, 1988.

HSE on the grounds that effective health and safety management depends on line managers taking primary responsibility for the health and safety of their employees. However, even within an advisory capacity the influence wielded by such safety personnel varies considerably from one organization to another. A crucial determinant of this has been found to be the degree of importance attached to health and safety by line managers, and senior management in particular.[21]

This last point serves to highlight a fundamental aspect of the management of health and safety, namely that decisions in the area are taken in the context of the resources and knowledge available within an organization, and the views, interests, power and priorities of the people involved in the decision-making process. Therefore, like other aspects of organizational decision-making, health and safety management has an important 'political' element. In effect, the legal framework relating to health and safety can be seen as a means by which society attempts, through moral pressure and financial penalties, to influence the relevant internal 'political' processes and the financial and other considerations informing them. The same is true of the actions taken by workers and their trade unions in the field, an issue to which attention now turns.

The role of work-force involvement

The issue of health and safety at work has formed an important part of the agenda of trade unions since their formation. The potentially valuable role of work-force involvement, whether through union or non-union channels, in raising the priority accorded to health and safety by employers and, more generally, contributing to the improvement of worker protection has long been recognized.[22] However, until the advent of the HSW Act no statutory provision was made for such involvement outside the coal-mining industry. As a result, the provision made for it depended on the attitudes of employer, workers and their unions, and the distribution of power between them.

This situation changed with the advent of the HSW Act. Under s.2 of this Act provisions were introduced which provided for the establishment of a statutory framework for employee representation. The provisions in question are to be found in s.2(4)–2(7) of the Act. Section 2(4) provides for regulations to be introduced enabling, in prescribed cases, the appointment by recognized trade unions of safety representatives from among employees to represent those employees in consultation with their employer.[23] Where such representatives are appointed, s.2(6) obliges employers to consult them with a view to co-operating effectively in promoting and developing measures to ensure the health and safety of employees. Finally, s.2(7) provides for regulations to require employers to establish a safety committee if requested to do so by representatives.

Regulations to activate s.2(4) and s.2(7), along with accompanying guidance notes and an approved code of practice, came into force on 1 October 1978. These regulations, the Safety Representatives and Safety Committees (SRSC) Regulations 1977, enable recognized unions, if they wish, to appoint one or more safety representatives from amongst employees.[23] Once appointed these representatives are provided with several 'functions': to investigate potential hazards and dangerous occurrences and to examine the causes of accidents; to investigate complaints relating to an employee's health, safety or welfare at work; to make representations to the employer on these and on general matters affecting the health, safety or welfare of employees; to carry out inspections in accordance with the regulations, including quarterly inspections of the work-place; to represent employees in consultations at the work-place with inspectors; to receive certain types of information from inspectors; and to attend meetings of safety committees. They are also given rights of paid time off to carry out these functions and to receive training. Finally, two or more representatives may ask an employer to establish a safety committee. For their part, employers are obliged to disclose certain types of information to employees and to provide them with such facilities and assistance as they may reasonably require.

The introduction of these regulations was seen by many to provide an important means through which employers could be encouraged to attach a higher priority to health and safety matters. Unfortunately, the research that has been conducted into their coverage and operation suggests that they have not had the positive effect originally envisaged by their proponents.

In terms of coverage, the available research findings suggest that the formal mechanisms for work-force involvement, although stimulated to some extent by the introduction of the regulations, apply to a small and diminishing proportion of British work-places. Findings from the 1990 work-place industrial relations survey, for example, suggest that just 23 per cent of work-places with twenty-five or more employees had joint health and safety committees, and only a further 9 per cent had joint committees which dealt partly with health and safety.[24] The survey did not specifically seek information on the presence of safety representatives, but did ask whether worker representatives of some sort existed in those work-places that did not possess safety committees. Only 24 per cent of establishments were found to do so, a figure considerably lower than the 41 per cent reported to have worker representatives in an earlier study (1984).

Moreover, case studies reveal a mixed picture regarding the effectiveness of safety representatives and safety committees. In work-places where union membership is high, trade unions are well organized and management adopts a supportive attitude, safety representatives and safety committee structures have been found to work well. However, in many other cases a far less satisfactory situation has been found, with only very partial application of the regulations being discovered.[25]

Such findings have led to a variety of proposals to improve the effectiveness and coverage of the SRSC Regulations. These fall into three broad categories.[26] First, the introduction of various amendments to the 1977 regulations, most notably to spell out more clearly the powers and duties of safety committees, to give safety representatives the right to stop hazardous work, to specify in greater detail the rights of representatives to undergo training and receive information, and to allow unions to appoint regional safety representatives. Secondly, the taking of steps to ensure more adequate enforcement of the Regulations by inspectors, possibly in conjunction with an entitlement to safety representatives to apply directly to the courts themselves. Thirdly, the introduction of statutory rights of involvement to work-places where unions are not recognized. It seems likely that a number of these reforms will be made should there be a change of government. Indeed, that regarding non-union representation may have to be introduced by the present government, because there are doubts whether the present 'union-only' channel of representation complies with the provisions of the EC framework directive on worker consultation.[27]

References

1. *Reporting of Injuries, Diseases and Dangerous Occurrences Regulations 1985* (SI 1985 No. 2023), London: HMSO.
2. *Health and Safety Commission annual report 1991/92*, London: HMSO.
3. *Employment Gazette* Occasional Supplement No. 3, September 1992.

4. Health and Safety Executive, *The Costs of Accidents at Work*, London: HMSO, 1993.
5. Harris, D., Maclean, M., Genn, H., Lloyd-Bostock, S., Fenn, P., Corfield, P. and Brittan, Y., *Compensation and Support for Illness and Injury*, Oxford: Clarendon, 1984.
6. Employers' Liability (Compulsory Insurance) Act 1964, London: HMSO.
7. Robens, Department of Employment. *Committee on Safety and Health at Work. Report of the Committee 1970–72*, Cmnd 5034, London: HMSO, 1972.
8. Woolf, A., 'Robens report: the wrong approach?', *Industrial Law Journal*, **2**, 1973, pp. 88–95.
9. James, P. and Lewis, D., 'Health and safety at work', in *Labour Law in Britain*, ed. Lewis, R., Oxford: Blackwell, 1986.
10. *Edwards v. National Coal Board* (1989) 1 KB 704.
11. James, P., *The European Community: a positive force for worker safety?*, London: Institute of Employment Rights, 1993.
12. See, for example, *Manual Handling Operations Regulations 1992* (SI 1992 No. 2793); *Health and Safety (Display Screen Equipment) Regulations 1992* (SI 1992 No. 2792), London: HMSO.
13. Council directive on the introduction of measures to encourage improvements in the safety and health of workers at the workplace (89/654/EEC).
14. *The Management of Health and Safety at Work Regulations 1992* (SI 1992 No. 2051).
15. Kay, H., 'Accidents: some facts and theories', in *Psychology at work* (2nd edn), ed. Warr, P. B., London: Penguin, 1978.
16. Nichols, T., 'Industrial injuries in British manufacturing in the 1980s – a commentary on Wright's article', *Sociological Review*, **34**(2), 1986, pp. 290–306; Dawson, S., Willman, P., Bamford, M. and Clinton, A., *Safety at Work: The limits of self-regulation*, Cambridge: CUP, 1988.
17. See, for example, Dept of Transport, *Investigation into the King's Cross Underground Fire*, London: HMSO, 1988; Dept of Transport, *Investigation into the Clapham Junction railway accident*, London: HMSO, 1989; and Dept of Energy, *The public inquiry into the Piper Alpha disaster*, London: HMSO, 1990.
18. Health and Safety Executive, *Monitoring safety*, London: HMSO, 1985.
19. Frick, K., 'Can management control health and safety?', *Economic and Industrial Democracy*, **11**, 1990, pp. 375–99.
20. Dawson *et al.*, *Safety at Work: The limits of self-regulation*.
21. *ibid.*
22. See Williams, J., *Accidents and Ill Health at Work*, London: Staple, 1960.
23. *Safety Representatives and Safety Committees Regulations 1977* (SI 1977 No. 500), London: HMSO.
24. Millward, N., Stevens, M., Smart, D. and Hawes, W. R., *Workplace Industrial Relations in Transition: the ED/ESRC/PSI/ACAS surveys*, Hampshire: Gower, 1992, Table 5.

25. See, for example, Dawson *et al.*, *Safety at Work: The limits of self-regulation*; Walters, D. and Gourlay, S., *Statutory Involvement in Health and Safety at the Workplace: A report of the implementation and effectiveness of the Safety Representatives and Safety Committees Regulations*, London: HSE, 1990.
26. See James, P., 'Reforming British health and safety law: a framework for discussion'. *Industrial Law Journal*, **21**(2), 1992, pp. 83–105.
27. *ibid.*

7

Trade unions and collective bargaining

Trade-union membership has declined significantly since 1979. The same is true of the coverage of collective bargaining. Nevertheless, unions and the process of union–management negotiation continue to play an important role in many organizations. Thus around 40 per cent of the work-force remain union members, while around 50 per cent of workers have their pay and conditions affected, either directly or indirectly, by collective bargaining.

This chapter commences with a brief introduction to the membership, structure and government of trade unions, and the main changes taking place in each of these areas. Attention then shifts to the role they play in regulating relationships with employers and the chief policy issues that employing organizations need to take into account when recognizing and dealing with trade unions.

Trade-union membership, structure and government

The origin of modern trade unions is the subject of historical debate.[1] For some their creation can be traced back to the craft guilds of the Middle Ages. For others, from sporadic combinations and associations of workers during the latter part of the seventeenth century. A point of agreement in both accounts, however, is that it was among skilled craft workers that trade-union organization first evolved.

Initially the early unions were restricted to particular geographical localities, and it was not until the mid-1850s, with the creation of what became known as the new model unions, that stable national unions were established. Even then, the union movement continued to be essentially a craft-based one. It was only with the rise of the new unionism at the end of the 1880s that widespread union organization developed among unskilled manual workers. Since then the fortunes of the union movement have fluctuated considerably, its membership going through periods of both substantial growth and decline.

Union membership nationally can be measured in absolute terms and as a proportion of potential union membership, commonly referred to as union density. Official figures on absolute membership, based on trade-union returns, are published for Britain by the Certification Office for Trade Unions and Employers' Associations and for the United Kingdom by the Department of Employment. Potential union membership is most frequently measured with reference to the size of the employed work-force plus the unemployed, although both narrower and broader measures are sometimes used: the employed work-force or the whole work-force (including the self-employed), but minus the armed forces. To complicate the matter further, estimates of union membership and density can also be based on the findings of various government-sponsored surveys.[2]

In density terms, six broad periods of union growth and decline can be distinguished for the United Kingdom during the twentieth century.[3] First, a period of steady growth to 1920, when union density reached 45.2 per cent. Secondly, a substantial slump in membership which ended in 1933 with union density at 22.6 per cent. Thirdly, another upsurge which peaked in 1948 with union density once again at 45.2 per cent. Fourthly, a period of stagnation and slight decline until 1968 when union density fell to 44 per cent. Fifthly, a decade of exceptional growth up to 1979 when density reached 55.4 per cent and absolute membership an all-time high of 13.4 million. Finally, a period of dramatic decline, resulting in a fall in density to less than 40 per cent.[4]

Considerable research has been carried out to identify the factors that have caused these fluctuations in union membership. Three broad categories of explanation can be identified.[5] One stresses the importance of changes in macro-economic variables such as wage inflation and unemployment. A second focuses on the role of structural change in the composition of the work-force; particular attention being paid here to sectoral shifts in the distribution of employment, and the changing balance in work-force composition between males and females, manual and non-manual work and full-time and part-time employment. The third explanation concentrates on changes in the industrial relations environment in which unions operate, looking at changes in the legislative framework, employers and union recognition, recruitment strategies and the effect of social norms on the decision to join a union.

Many of these variables are, of course, interrelated. Employer policies towards union recognition, for example, are likely to be influenced by trends in unemployment and government legislation. Partly because of this, considerable uncertainty still remains as to the relative weight that should be attached to the different types of explanation put forward. What is clear, however, is that the environment facing unions today contains a variety of features that are not conducive to the maintenance, or for that matter the growth, of trade-union membership. These include, a government that, as both an employer and legislator, is committed to a reduction in trade-union power; a continued and long-term shift away from sectors of employment such as manufacturing, which have long traditions of union organization, towards the less well-organized private services; a parallel and related growth of non-manual, part-time and temporary work; and the presence, since 1979, of high levels of unemployment by post-war standards and, for most of this period, low inflation and rising real wages. To these may be added a far greater reluctance on the part of employers to recognize, and in some cases continue to recognize, trade unions.

Views as to future trends in union membership, because of the uncertainty surrounding the relative importance of these various factors, inevitably differ to some extent. Some analysts argue that the recent decline in union membership constitutes part of a long-term process of decline which will ultimately lead to membership levels similar to those in the United States, which currently stand at around 15 per cent. Others are more optimistic and suggest that an improved economic performance and/or the election of a government more sympathetic to the union movement could act to halt, if not reverse, the present decline.

Meanwhile, in the absence of such favourable shifts, unions have been adopting a range of initiatives designed to make them more attractive to current and potential members. In addition to campaigning for the election of a Labour government, these include campaigns designed to recruit new members in the fastest-growing industries and among previously neglected groups, such as women and part-timers; improved services to members, such as improved legal advice and the provision of various financial services; and attempts to adapt their policies and role better to appeal to non-unionists.[6]

At present relatively little evidence is available as to the effectiveness of these various initiatives, and considerable disagreement exists as to their likely success. In the case of recruitment, for example, two main schools of thought can be distinguished. The first casts severe doubt on the extent to which unions can do much to improve aggregate union membership until favourable changes take place in the broader social and economic environment,[7] while the second argues that this viewpoint considerably underestimates the role that union leadership can play in encouraging union membership growth.[8]

No definitive answer can be given to the correctness of these two schools of thought. However, the more optimistic perspective does face the problem of whether unions have the resources available to mount effective recruitment campaigns in a climate where employers are generally hostile to giving unions recognition. Union membership fees in Britain are, and always have been, low by international standards and an important consequence of this is that the ratio of full-time officials to members is also very low in most of the larger unions. As a result, such officials often have more than enough to do in servicing existing members, let alone taking an active part in recruitment exercises. This, in turn, highlights a crucial dilemma that faces unions in considering how to improve member recruitment – namely how this can be done in a way that does not have a detrimental effect on the resources made available to support existing members.[9]

Certainly many current recruitment campaigns are apparently not very well co-ordinated or monitored at the centre, and place considerable responsibility on local lay representatives or shop stewards for carrying them out.[10] This reliance on local union activists has its advantages, since Trades Union Congress (TUC) research indicates that there are up to 2 million non-unionists employed in work-places where unions are recognized, although a substantial number of these may well be very reluctant unionists. It does, however, mean that much recruitment activity is likely to be focused on sectors of industry where unions are already well organized rather than in those sectors where union membership is low but employment is growing.

Trade-union structure

In 1990 union membership in the United Kingdom was distributed between 287 different unions, a figure that includes employer-based staff associations which fulfil the statutory qualification for registration as a trade union: that is a body not under the domination or control of an employer.[11] These unions differed considerably with regard to size. Thus the smallest, the Johnson Matthey Staff Association, had just two members, while the largest, the Transport and General Workers' Union (TGWU), had a membership of 1 223 891. However, the majority of union members (59 per cent) belonged to just nine unions.

Only a minority of trade unions (72 in 1992) belong to the TUC, but these include most of the largest unions in the country. As a result, in 1992 around 80 per cent of union members belonged to TUC-affiliated organizations.

British unions differ considerably in terms of both the types of workers they represent and the sectors of industry in which those members work. Unfortunately, it is far from easy to go much beyond this in terms of describing the structure of the British union movement without examining in detail the actual composition and recruitment activities of individual unions, because of the complex differences which exist between them in terms of how they define their 'membership markets'.

Traditionally, three types of union have been distinguished: craft, industrial and general. However, while of use as a means of classifying the origins and early aspirations of unions, this schema has never coped particularly well with the complex patterns of recruitment that have characterized the British union movement. Even at the end of the nineteenth century, there were no industrial unions in the full sense of the term, that is unions recruiting among all categories of worker in a particular industry as happens in Germany, and unions described as general have never recruited on as wide a basis as the term implies, being from the outset essentially 'residual' in their recruitment activities: that is, filling in gaps left by occupational unions and those with industrial aspirations which had existed prior to the development of general unionism at the end of the 1880s.[12]

Developments during the twentieth century have further undermined the descriptive value of this traditional approach to union classification, even if the additional categories of white-collar or occupational unions are added. Craft unionism, the category that could be applied least problematically to the British union movement in the nineteenth century, is now no longer an important feature of the movement: the few pure craft unions remaining being insignificant in terms of membership. Industrial unionism, in the sense of unions restricting recruitment to a single industry, has similarly become of less, rather than more, importance over the course of the century, while most of the largest unions now include both manual and non-manual workers.

The failure of this traditional system of classification to describe current union structures is not surprising. British unions have never sought to define their areas of recruitment in terms of abstract principles, but instead have seen the issue as forming an integral part of the strategies needed to further the interests of their members and themselves in the context of the broader social, economic and political environment in which they operate. Consequently, unions have tended to adjust their approaches to recruitment in response to changes in this broader environment. Craft unionism, for example, is now of relatively little importance, but not because it was rejected as a basis of organization *per se*. Rather, its demise reflects the fact that this form of organization, based as it is on the maintenance of control over the supply of labour, became increasingly untenable in the face of technological change and shifts in the occupational and sectoral composition of industry.

In other words, the boundaries of union recruitment activities have evolved to cope with the environment in which unions operate, in much the same way as business organizations have adapted their activities and structures to deal with changes in consumer demand and market competition. Indeed there are striking parallels between how unions and commercial trading companies have adjusted their recruitment and business strategies. Thus, as industry has become increasingly dominated by large conglomerates with interests in a variety of industrial sectors, so unions, partly in response to this trend, have become increasingly open in their recruitment policies, with the result that their memberships are now far more diverse in terms of the jobs that members do and the sectors in which they do them. Consequently, most of the country's largest unions now embody elements of more than one of the types of union distinguished in the traditional classification of union structure.

These more open patterns of recruitment have evolved through a combination of internally driven adjustments of recruitment territories and mergers between unions. However, the latter source of change has been the more important because of the limited scope that unions have had to expand their traditional job territories, as a result of two interrelated factors. First, the presence of other unions in sectors where they might otherwise like to have expanded. Secondly, the role that TUC rules on interunion relations have played in protecting the interests of those already established unions.

The TUC first laid down rules governing union recruitment activities in 1924. These were subsequently amended and extended at its 1939 Bridlington congress, and since then have traditionally been referred to as the Bridlington principles. These principles, which have themselves been amended on a number of occasions, lay down restrictions in respect of two main types of recruitment activity: the 'poaching' of members from one union by another; and the commencement of 'organizing activities' by unions in organizations where another union has an 'interest'. Where a union feels that another union has contravened the principles, it may submit a formal complaint to the TUC. Ultimately, a Disputes Committee can be set up to consider the case and make an award. A failure to comply with such an award can lead to a union's suspension and eventual expulsion from the TUC. Expulsion has been used relatively rarely, the most recent example being that of the then Electrical, Electronic, Telecommunications, and Plumbing Union (EETPU) in 1988 for failing to comply with an instruction to withdraw from two single-union agreements.

Union mergers take one of two forms – amalgamations, where two or more unions combine together to form a new one, and transfers of engagements, where one union takes over the membership of another. Such mergers, which like their company equivalents may occur for expansionist, consolidatory or defensive reasons,[13] have been a continuing feature of the union movement over the past century, although the scale of merger activity has varied from one time period to another. Their occurrence, for example, does much to explain the reason why the number of unions in Britain has declined from the 1920 peak figure of 1384.

This process of union concentration through merger is very much in evidence today. A number of important mergers have taken place in recent years, most notably the amalgamation of the Association of Scientific, Technical, and Managerial Staffs (ASTMS) and the Technical, Administrative, and Supervisory Section (TASS) of the Amalgamated Engineering Union (AEU) to create the Manufacturing, Science and Finance Union (MSF), and the coming together of the AEU and the EETPU to form the Amalgamated Engineering and Electrical Union (AEEU). Moreover, a variety of others are at various stages of discussion. The three public-sector unions, the National

Union of Public Employees (NUPE), the National and Local Government Officers' Association (NALGO) and the Confederation of Health Service Employees (COHSE) are, for example, in the midst of finalizing an amalgamation which will, at least for the time being, overtake the TGWU as the largest union in the country. Meanwhile, the TGWU itself has opened merger discussions with the General, Municipal, Boilermakers and Allied Trades Union (GMB) which, if successful, would enable it – albeit as a constituent part of a new union – to establish itself once again as the country's biggest union.

The number of mergers currently under discussion indicates that this process of expanding membership territories through acquisition will continue to exert an important influence over the structure of the union movement for the rest of this century. Indeed, it seems highly likely that by the turn of the century the vast majority of union members will belong to a mere handful of union conglomerates whose interests spread over a massive range of occupations and industrial sectors. The structural changes that will flow from these mergers are, moreover, likely to be compounded by the greater freedom which TUC unions are likely to have in the future to define their recruitment areas, as the result of new legislative provisions which give current or prospective unionists a right of complaint to an industrial tribunal where they are excluded or expelled from a union on the grounds that their recruitment involved breaching the TUC's Bridlington principles.[14]

Union government

Four features are common to the governmental structures of the larger unions: a national representative conference held annually, or in a few cases biannually; an executive body, often called the National Executive; some form of branch organization; and a chief officer, usually titled General Secretary but sometimes President.

The precise form of these four elements of government varies considerably between unions, as does the balance of power existing between them. Delegates to union conferences, for example, may be elected by branches, as in the case of the TGWU, or less commonly by some form of divisional or regional body which itself consists of branch delegates – a practice adopted in the engineering section of the AEEU. Similarly, while the role of conferences is invariably that of reviewing the work of the union and discussing and determining national policy, in unions characterized by large, heterogeneous memberships the discussion of negotiations and settlements in particular industries may be excluded from remit of conferences, since discussions of this type will be irrelevant to many of the delegates present. Where this is the case, separate trade- or industry-based conferences are frequently used to enable such issues to be discussed at national level.

Branch organization also exhibits marked variation. Three broad types of branch can be distinguished – geographical, work-place and single-employer – and the use made of these varies between unions. Geographical branches may be run by full-time secretaries, but more frequently this role is occupied by lay representatives, i.e. union activists not employed by the union. In either case the majority of branch committee members are likely to be shop stewards from work-places falling within the geographical area covered by the branch.

Until recently a variety of different methods were employed to appoint union executives and chief officers. However, as a result of government legislation passed in the 1980s all such appointments must now be made by means of secret postal ballots conducted every five years.[15] The constituencies used for balloting purposes are defined on different bases. Constituencies may, for example, be defined on geographical or trade/industry lines. In addition, different constituent sections of the union may be entitled, again on geographical or trade/industry basis, to appoint their own members of the executive. To confuse the matter even further, a number of unions have in recent years decided to reserve a number of executive seats for women in an attempt to improve the representation of female members. A case in point is Unison, the union to be created as a result of the merger of COHSE, NUPE and NALGO, where thirteen of the places on the executive are to be reserved for women.

Chief officers in the large unions occupy their post on a full-time, salaried basis for the duration of their appointment. Executive members may, however, be full-time employees or lay representatives – although the latter may, in practice, be full-time shop stewards who have been released from their normal work duties to carry out union functions. Both of these approaches have potential advantages and disadvantages. The practice of full-time appointment may enable those concerned to carry out their work more efficiently and to keep a closer eye on the activities of the union's chief officer. On the other hand, it does carry the danger that executive members may be less in touch with the experiences, views and aspirations of those they have been appointed to represent. A similar issue of accountability arises over whether it is better to appoint or elect full-time officials, i.e. the members of staff who carry out much of the day-to-day representative work of the union.

The issue of union democracy more generally has been the subject of long-standing debate. Two main themes have dominated this debate. First, how far and in what ways union members exert effective control over their leaders. Secondly, whether and to what extent it is legitimate for the government to intervene in the internal decision-making arrangements of unions.

The most pessimistic view of union democracy is that, for a variety of organizational reasons, unions inevitably tend towards oligarchic control by a small group of senior officials.[16] A good deal of evidence concerning the actual practice of union government would appear to lend weight to this view. Doubts can, for example, be expressed about the ability of union executives and conferences to exert control over the actions of their chief officers, given the way in which some general secretaries have been able at various times to exercise considerable power over union policies. Attention can also be drawn to the way in which the agenda of union conferences and the debates that take place can be manipulated by the 'platform', and the generally low attendance, often considerably less than 10 per cent, achieved at branch meetings.

In considering such criticisms, however, care must be taken not to underestimate the ability of union members to keep their leaders in check by both constitutional and other means. The constitutions of many of the larger unions, for example, embody a degree of devolution or separation of powers that acts to circumscribe severely the extent of oligarchic control that can be exercised by senior officials. In addition, members have a variety of less formal means of making their views and dissatisfaction known to union officials. These include: individual and collective resignations, the formation of breakaway unions, the use of pressure groups and factions and non-compliance with union policies.[17]

On balance, it is therefore highly misleading to view unions as being characterized by oligarchic control. Nevertheless, it does not follow from this that the internal democracy of unions is beyond reproach. Certainly, this has not been the view of successive Conservative governments since 1979.

During this period, a range of legislation has been introduced with the explicit aim of shifting the balance of power away from union leaders to their members. The requirements on union elections already referred to are a case in point. Other examples include: provisions that make the closed shop legally unenforceable, the introduction of requirements for ballots before industrial action, the obligation on unions to conduct ballots every ten years on the maintenance of political funds, and the giving to union members of a right of complaint if particular types of 'unjustifiable discipline' are taken against them.[18]

The introduction of these legislative controls has been the subject of considerable controversy, both in terms of their actual requirements and whether it is legitimate for governments to interfere in the internal government of unions. Both of these lines of criticism can be illustrated by reference to the requirements on the use of postal ballots to elect those attending union executive meetings.

Postal ballots have been advocated by the government on three main grounds: as a means of securing higher levels of participation in the appointment of union leaders, as a vehicle for overcoming the administrative weaknesses and potential malpractices associated with branch and work-place ballots, and as a way of enabling members to vote in the privacy of their homes and hence in the absence of pressures from other union members. The validity of each of these arguments has been challenged.[19] Two particular counter-arguments merit mention. The first is that the passive nature of postal balloting, by limiting the extent to which issues can be explained and discussed at meetings, reduces rather than improves the quality of union democracy. The second challenges the argument that it encourages higher levels of participation in elections, on the grounds that while postal ballots can lead to higher turnouts than voting through branch meetings, the opposite is true when they are compared to the turnouts obtained through work-place ballots.

This last point has led some to argue that the government's legislation has been less concerned with improving democracy and more with ensuring that unions behave in the way that the government wants them to. Inevitably this interpretation has been rejected by government. The potential for legislation to be used in this way does, however, raise important questions about the role of democracy in unions and the right of governments to interfere in their internal electoral arrangements.

Any government legislation on union democracy involves, by definition, placing limits on the ability of unions to develop systems of government which they consider to best suit their own needs and circumstances. The provisions on postal balloting, for example, has forced some unions to abolish the practice of appointing rather than electing chief officers; has required others to move away from using work-place and branch ballots; and has required yet others to abolish arrangements whereby executive committee members were elected by delegates to annual conference. In some cases it can be argued that the changes unions have made in response to the legislative requirements have, indeed, served to increase member influence over union decision-making. In others the opposite would seem to have happened.[20] In either case, however, it does not necessarily follow that members have benefited overall from the changes made.

The primary function of trade unions is to protect and further the interests of their members. Democratic accountability is an important feature of their governmental structures, because it provides a means through which union leaders can be made aware of members' views and aspirations and a mechanism by which members can ensure that due account is taken of them. Such accountability is therefore essentially functional, in the sense that it constitutes a means to an end rather than an end in itself.

This distinction between means and ends is an important one, because it highlights a crucial point about union constitutions – namely that all embody some form of compromise between the desire for democratic control, on the one hand, and the needs of efficiency of service to members, on the other. The precise form of this compromise inevitably varies from one union to another as a result of a whole host of historical, philosophical and environmental influences. Government legislation designed to improve union democracy may therefore achieve this objective, but at the cost of damaging the effectiveness with which a union is able to protect and further the interests of its members. Whether, and to what extent, such adverse consequences do arise will, of course, depend on the nature of the legislation introduced. The potential for it to have this effect clearly raises major issues of political policy over how far it is legitimate for a government to interfere in the internal running of independent trade unions.

Management–union relations

Union membership is not distributed evenly through the economy. The same is true of union recognition by employers.

Figures from the 1991 Labour Force Survey show union density to vary from 71 per cent in the energy and water supply industries, to 36 per cent and 33 per cent in the manufacturing and services sectors, respectively.[21] Moreover, these broad sectoral differences encompass significant variations in membership between different constituent industries. This is particularly true of the services sector, where membership density ranges from 92 per cent in the railways to 9 per cent in business services.

The 1990 work-place industrial relations survey shows that 48 per cent of work-places with twenty-five or more employees recognized unions for manual workers and 43 per cent did so for non-manual workers.[22] However, these aggregate figures need to be treated with caution for two reasons. First, because they undoubtedly overstate the extent of recognition in the economy as a whole by excluding small work-places where union density and recognition, at least outside of the public sector, tends to be low – a fact that reflects the more general positive relationship that exists in the private sector between numbers employed and these two measures of union organization. Secondly, because they conceal significant differences in recognition between different sectors of the economy (see Table 7.1).

The similarities that exist in the patterns of union recognition and density reflect the mutually reinforcing relationship between these two phenomena. Thus, on the one hand, high (low) union membership may well make employers more (less) responsive to union requests for recognition. On the other hand, the presence or absence of employer recognition, as noted earlier in the section on union membership, is likely to impact on the willingness of workers to join and remain in unions.[23]

Employer attitudes towards recognition are influenced by a variety of considerations. On the negative side, union organization may be resisted on the grounds that their recognition will involve management having to concede some of its freedom to determine unilaterally how work is organized and the terms and conditions on which workers are employed. This infringement of managerial prerogatives may, in turn, be seen to have potentially harmful consequences for labour costs and productivity. More generally, the presence of unions may be opposed because it is feared that their presence may serve to damage management–worker relationships and involve considerable amounts of management time being tied up on negotiating and consulting with unions. On the positive side, unions may be seen to provide a valuable channel of communication with the work-force. Collective bargaining may also be considered a useful means of gaining work-force commitment, particularly to change, and an efficient way of altering the employment contracts of large numbers of staff simultaneously.

The weight attached to these various arguments is inevitably influenced by a variety of historical, environmental and philosophic-

Table 7.1 Trade union recognition, by broad sector, 1980, 1984 and 1990 (percentages)

	All establishments			Private manufacturing			Private services			Public sector		
	1980	1984	1990	1980	1984	1990	1980	1984	1990	1980	1984	1990
Establishments with recognized trade unions for manual workers:												
as a proportion of all establishments	55	62	48	65	55	44	33	38	31	76	91	78
as a proportion of establishments with manual union members	86	91	83	85	85	77	80	81	76	92	99	91
Establishments with recognized trade unions for non-manual workers:												
as a proportion of all establishments	47	54	43	27	26	23	28	30	26	91	98	84
as a proportion of establishments with non-manual union members	87	92	84	74	75	89	82	85	80	93	99	85
Establishments with recognized trade unions for any workers:												
as a proportion of all establishments	64	66	53	65	56	44	41	44	36	94	99	87
as a proportion of establishments with any union members	88	91	83	84	83	77	81	82	78	95	99	89

Source: Millward, N. *et al.*, *Workplace Industrial Relations in Transition: The ED/ESRC/PSI/ACAS surveys*, Aldershot: Gower, 1992.

al considerations. Developments in other employing organizations, past experiences of dealing with unions, and the attitudes of government towards unions, as demonstrated by its approach to unionism as an employer and a legislator, are all likely to exert important influences over employer policies. The personal philosophy of key managers is also likely to play an important role.

Unfortunately, the evidence available on what impact unions do have on pay levels and organizational efficiency is the subject of considerable debate, and it is far from easy to reach any definitive conclusions.[24] What is clear, as noted earlier, is that employers since the end of the 1970s have been far less willing to recognize unions and, in a relatively small number of cases, actually derecognized them – either across an organization as a whole or among particular occupational groups and locations.[25] This shift in employer attitudes, when combined with the structural shifts in the economy away from those sectors such as manufacturing, where union membership is well established, to those where it isn't, such as retailing, has resulted in a decline in the proportion of work-places where unions are recognized (see Table 7.1).

This is not to say that unions have not managed to secure any new recognition agreements during this period. That would be to overstate the case. A number of single-union agreements have, for example, been signed with Japanese transplants which have started up operations on greenfield sites. Rather it is to say that the frequency of such agreements has been insufficient to counteract the forces that are working in the opposite direction.

Where unions are recognized, the structure and nature of the relationships established with employers vary considerably. Some of the more important of these differences can usefully be outlined by considering in turn four issues: the nature and role of work-place union organization; the scope of recognition; the structure of collective bargaining arrangements; and the nature of collective agreements.

Work-place union organization

In a substantial, although declining, proportion of work-places where unions are recognized, representatives have been elected by members from among their number (see Table 7.2). These representatives are customarily referred to as shop stewards, although in some unions they may have different titles. For example, they are called staff representatives in some white-collar unions, and father or mother of the chapel in the print industry.

Table 7.2 Presence of trade-union representatives, by broad sector, 1984 and 1990 (percentages)

	All establishments		Private manufacturing		Private services		Public sector	
	1984	1990	1984	1990	1984	1990	1984	1990
Manual or non-manual workers represented by:								
1 or more representatives at own work place	82	71	98	90	67	57	84	73
Representatives elsewhere in organization	29	26	3	3	20	23	42	37
Full-time union official	8	14	1	7	11	12	10	17
Senior representative of 2 or more present	19	22	46	40	9	12	14	23
Full-time representative present	2	2	5	2	1	2	3	2
Base: establishments with recognized unions for manual or non-manual workers								

Source: Millward, N. *et al.*, *Workplace Industrial Relations in Transition: The ED/ESRC/PSI/ACAS surveys*, Aldershot: Gower, 1992.

In carrying out their duties, shop stewards are subject to pressures from three directions: the managers with whom they deal, their members and the national union to which they belong. The nature of these demands inevitably conflicts to some extent, with the result that the stewards' role can be far from a comfortable one. This, together with the fact that their role may have adverse consequences for job and career prospects, and that they have to give up considerable amounts of leisure time, helps to explain why, although stewards are generally subject to periodic re-election, it is relatively uncommon for there to be alternative candidates.

The precise role played by stewards varies considerably between work-places and employing organizations. In broad terms, their functions can be divided into two. First, carrying out negotiating and representative functions on behalf of members, and, secondly, providing administrative support to the national union.

Shop stewards play a crucial role in the day-to-day running of unions. They are responsible for recruiting new members and ensuring that existing ones remain in membership. They are also expected to act as guardians of official union policy at the work-place and they provide an important channel of communication between members and the wider union. Stewards, for example, generally attend branch meetings more frequently than ordinary members, as well as playing an important part in the administration of these meetings, and often distribute union journals and other forms of union communication. In addition, they sometimes have responsibility for collecting union subscriptions, although the widespread use of the 'check off', the arrangement whereby union dues are deducted directly from pay by employers, means that this function is less important than in the past.

Stewards use a variety of different forms of argument to protect and advance the interests of their members, and may also threaten and seek to employ one or more forms of collective action, including strikes, overtime bans, go-slows and work-to-rules (see Chapter 9). In practice, the power they wield through these methods will be influenced by such factors as the extent and nature of their membership, the sophistication of the work-place union organization and the broader environment in which they operate, notably the legal framework relating to industrial relations, the level of unemployment in the economy and their sector of industry, their bargaining power, and the trading and financial position of the employing organization.

The membership represented by stewards can vary considerably in terms of their general attitudes to the employment relationship and the potential power they are able to exercise *vis-à-vis* the employer. Shop stewards can, similarly, differ markedly in terms of their own attitudes and negotiating experience and skills, and the relationships they have with members and managers. They can also adopt very different approaches to their role. One study carried out in the car industry, for example, drew a distinction between 'leader' and 'populist' stewards.[26] Leaders were found to play an active role in shaping claims, sometimes to the point of rejecting issues raised by members, and determining the tactics to be employed in pursuance of them. Populists, in contrast, tended to see their role more as delegates whose task was to pursue all items raised by members. A significant point emerging from the study was that leaders were frequently far more effective in their dealings with managers. At the same time their tactical acumen and ability to influence members meant that they often acted to introduce a greater degree of stability and predictability into management–union relations – a finding which serves to highlight the point that 'weak' stewards are not necessarily desirable as far as employers are concerned.

Shop-steward organizations exhibit marked differences in terms of their sophistication. In larger work-places senior stewards, or convenors, are frequently appointed to co-ordinate the activities of their colleagues and act as a source of advice and guidance. Shop-steward committees, consisting of stewards from one or more unions, may also be formed (see below), and in multi-establishment organizations, combined committees may be formed to bring together representatives from the different work-places within the enterprise.

Employers frequently make a range of facilities available to shop stewards. Statutory provisions require them to disclose certain types of information to union officials for collective-bargaining purposes and to provide them with time off to receive training and carry out their industrial relations duties.[27] Some organizations, however, go considerably beyond these minimum requirements. In addition, in some work-places union convenors are given full release from their normal work activities, and it is common for stewards to be given access to a range of administrative resources, such as a union office, telephone, secretarial support and access to photocopying.

Scope of recognition

Union recognition can be limited to the representation of workers, either individually or collectively, in grievance and disciplinary matters, or extend to negotiations over terms and conditions of employment. The types of workers covered by these recognition agreements may also differ. Thus, in some organizations they may apply only to manual workers, while in others non-manual staff may also be covered. Similarly, the seniority of staff to which recognition applies varies, particularly between the public and private sectors. In general, union membership and recognition are relatively uncommon among all but the most junior levels of management in the private sector, whereas the opposite is the case in such parts of the public sector as local authorities and the National Health Service.

Collective bargaining between employers and unions can encompass a vast array of issues: hours of work, holidays, staffing levels, payment systems, pensions, gradings, redeployment, physical working conditions, job content and pay are just some of the topics that may be covered. The subjects encompassed by bargaining have frequently been divided into two broad categories: those that deal with 'market' relations, that is basic terms and conditions of workers, and those that relate to the internal operation or 'government' of an organization. Historically, employers have been far less willing to concede negotiating rights in respect of matters falling within the latter area, and the extent of negotiation over such issues has formed a crucial indicator of where the 'frontier of control' between employers and workers resides in particular organizations.

The actual subjects covered by collective bargaining vary considerably from one organization to another, for a whole host of organizational, technological and economic reasons. In general, the 1970s were characterized by a gradual extension of the range of negotiable matters. Since then the available evidence suggests that the bargaining agenda has tended to narrow in many organizations – sometimes dramatically – against a background of declining union membership and power.[28] This decline in union influence has in turn enabled employers to introduce wide-ranging changes to existing collective agreements.

Grading structures have been simplified to remove restrictive demarcations between different categories of jobs, sometimes as part of harmonization programmes intended to abolish unnecessary distinctions in the terms and conditions of manual and non-manual workers. Closer links have been established between pay and performance through various forms of merit pay and profit sharing. Working practices have been reformed to achieve greater labour flexibility by, for example, breaking down demarcations between different types of craft worker and making production workers responsible for inspecting the quality of their work and carrying out routine maintenance. Working hours have also been reformed, and greater use made of part-time, temporary and sub-contract staff to obtain a better match between labour supply and demand. New patterns of working hours to emerge include the use of 'min-max' contracts, under which employers are able to vary the number of hours an employee works during a particular week up to a specified maximum, and annual hours schemes, which enable the number of hours worked in a defined period to be varied in relation to a given number of working hours per year.[29]

Structure of bargaining

The structure of collective bargaining can be analyzed for present purposes along two interrelated dimensions. First, the number of separate bargaining units present and, secondly, the level at which bargaining takes place.

A bargaining unit refers to the types of workers covered by a given set of negotiations. In some organizations there may be only one such unit. However, in many organizations more than one unit exists. For example, manual and non-manual groups may be covered by separate sets of negotiations, and within the manual work-force different agreements may be concluded in respect of skilled workers and their unskilled and semi-skilled colleagues. Similarly, different bargaining units may exist for different geographical parts of an organization's operations, or for different types of business activity.

The presence of different bargaining units for different occupational groups is intimately connected to the historical development of trade-union organization in Britain and the traditional patterns of representation to which this has given rise. As noted previously, the recruitment patterns of unions have encompassed horizontal, occupational-based approaches, vertical, industry-based strategies and 'residual' general ones. An important consequence of this has been that their areas of recruitment have exhibited a considerable degree of overlap, both in occupational and industrial terms. This, in turn, has resulted in many organizations recognizing and dealing with a number of different unions, particularly in the public sector (see Table 7.3). The extent and nature of this multiunionism, as it is known, differ. In some cases it involves a number of unions being present, each of which is recognized in respect of a particular occupational group. In others, it may involve several unions being recognized to represent the same groups of workers.

Table 7.3   Numbers of recognized unions, 1990 (percentages)

	Any unions	Manual only	Non-manual only	Mixed
None	–	46	37	64
1	36	40	33	29
2	31	9	15	5
3	12	4	5	1
4 or more	20	2	9	
Mean	2.5	0.8	1.3	0.45

Source: Millward, N. *et al.*, *Workplace Industrial Relations in Transition: The ED/ESRC/PSI/ACAS surveys*, Aldershot: Gower, 1992.

Multiunionism has frequently been criticized for the harmful consequences it has for both industrial relations and the internal efficiency of organizations more generally. It can give rise to interunion disputes over recruitment and demarcation issues, generate competitive bargaining between the different unions, complicate the collective bargaining process because of the need to reach agreements that are acceptable to each of the union groups, and lead to much management and union time being tied up in concluding different agreements for different groups of workers. However, it does have certain potential advantages for both unions and employers. Employers, for example, may be able to exploit the situation by playing one union group against another, and it may enable them to keep union attention focused on more parochial issues and hence away from matters of more strategic significance to the organization as a whole. For workers, it can provide them with union representation more closely attuned to their own occupational interests and, possibly, can allow improvements in terms and conditions to be secured through the use of comparability arguments.

Both unions and employers have developed various strategies to avoid, or at least limit, the potential harmful consequences of multiunionism. The TUC's Bridlington principles were, for example, developed with the express intention of helping to avoid and resolve interunion conflict over recruitment and organizing activities (see above). Various TUC committees have also been set up to bring together unions in the same industry to discuss issues of common interest. Below the level of the TUC, unions have formed federations in particular sectors and signed spheres of influence agreements intended to clarify their respective areas of interest in particular sectors and organizations. Union mergers have also, albeit often as a by-product, done much to reduce the scale of multiunionism and/or the problems arising from it.

Joint bargaining arrangements, under which a number of unions come together to bargain with employers, have been developed as a means of reducing the number of separate agreements that need to be concluded. In the past, these arrangements have frequently been partial, in the sense that they applied only to some of the unions present and, in particular, have rarely brought together unions representing manual and non-manual workers. In recent years, however, a number of employers have been seeking to extend such arrangements, in some cases going so far as to establish 'single-table' bargaining machinery, which brings together all unions within the organization. The desire to achieve the types of benefits obtained by those companies that have signed single-union agreements on greenfield sites over the past decade has been an important factor encouraging this trend. Another has been the felt need to adjust bargaining arrangements in a way that will assist moves towards harmonizing the terms and conditions of manual and non-manual staff in such areas as payment systems, sick pay and holidays. Yet another has been the perceived value of such machinery in helping with the introduction of new working practices, which blur traditional boundaries between job categories and grades.

The level at which collective bargaining takes place will also often influence the number and nature of bargaining units. Collective bargaining can take place at industry level, where employers combine together through the medium of employers' associations, as well as in individual organizations. Within individual organizations it can take place at a number of different levels, the most important being the organization as a whole, the division and the establishment or work-place. Table 7.4, taken from the 1990 workplace industrial relations survey, shows the relative importance of these different levels of bargaining.

Industry-wide bargaining is of declining importance, and has been throughout the post-war period. However, it continues to operate in a number of sectors, including electrical contracting, construction, local government and transport. Where industry-level bargaining continues to take place, it generally – at least outside of the public sector – sets only minimum rates of pay, which are often considerably enhanced as a result of negotiations conducted within individual organizations. Industry-wide terms concerning matters such as overtime premia, sick pay, hours of work and holidays are, in contrast, usually followed.

Table 7.4   Basis for most recent pay increase, all sectors, 1980, 1984 and 1990 (percentages)

	Manual employees			Non-manual employees		
	1980	1984	1990	1980	1984	1990
Result of collective bargaining	55	62	48	47	54	43
Most important level:						
Multi-employer	32	40	26	29	36	24
Single employer, multi-plant	12	13	13	11	13	15
Plant/establishment	9	7	6	4	4	3
Other answer	1	1	2	2	1	1

Base: establishments with employees named in column heads

Source: Millward, N. *et al.*, *Workplace Industrial Relations in Transition: The ED/ESRC/PSI/ACAS surveys*, Aldershot: Gower, 1992.

Until recently the trend away from multi-employer, industry-wide bargaining was essentially a private-sector one. However, it is now also apparent in the public sector. For example, a number of local authorities have broken away from the national agreement for white-collar staff and this trend seems likely to continue.[30] The setting up of National Health Service (NHS) trusts is having a similar effect in the NHS.

The continued movement away from multi-employer bargaining has primarily reflected a desire on the part of employers to have greater freedom to develop pay and reward systems that more closely meet their operational and labour market needs – although political pressures have also played an important role in the public sector. Such considerations have prompted many organizations to re-appraise the appropriateness of their existing domestic negotiating arrangements during the past decade or so. In a growing number of cases this process of re-appraisal has led companies to decide to decentralize their bargaining machinery down to the divisional or work-place level. Lucas, Phillips, Royal Insurance, Courtaulds and Pilkington are just a few of the companies that have gone down this route in recent years.[31]

Centralized and decentralized bargaining arrangements both have potential advantages and disadvantages. Centralized arrangements can make labour costs more predictable, enable a common approach to be adopted towards union recognition and ensure that negotiations are carried out by skilled and experienced negotiators. They can also, by enabling the establishment of common terms and conditions, facilitate the transfer of staff between different parts of an organization and ensure consistency between work-places, thereby avoiding jealousies and rivalries between staff at different locations. On the other hand, central negotiations can be very time consuming and lead to delays in resolving disputes. They also tend to mean that pay rates have to be set at a level sufficient to recruit in the most expensive labour markets in which the employer is operating. In addition, it can be rather difficult in such negotiations to take account of differences in the performance of different work-places and the types of work they carry out, and to engage in detailed discussions of ways of improving efficiency. A further potential problem is that when negotiations break down, any resultant disputes are likely to affect the whole organization rather than just one part of its operations.

The significance attached to these different advantages and disadvantages will be influenced by a variety of factors. Some of the more important of these are usefully highlighted in Table 7.5. As can be seen, they include internal management structures, existing patterns of union representation and collective bargaining, the types of payment systems in use, the geographical spread of work-places, the nature of labour and product markets, and the types of work carried out in them. However, three sets of considerations appear to have been central to recent moves to establish more decentralized arrangements.[32] First, a change in corporate strategy and business policy towards local profit centres. Secondly, a desire to establish closer links between pay and performance. Thirdly, a number of legal and environmental changes which have acted both to reduce the effectiveness of union opposition to such moves and lessen the threat to employers of comparability-based pay claims. These changes have included relatively high levels of unemployment, falling union membership and power, and the introduction of legal restrictions that limit the ability of unions to initiate organization-wide strikes in situations where bargaining arrangements are decentralized.

It must be stressed that not all organizations are decentralizing collective bargaining. This is particularly true of 'critical function' companies and those who continue to have centralized systems of financial and management control.[33] Moreover, those organizations that are decentralizing are not necessarily doing so for all groups of workers. In multiple retailing, for example, some employers have decided to decentralize their negotiations in respect of distribution staff, while leaving the determination of pay for sales personnel on a centralized basis.

Table 7.5 Decentralization planning checklist

Corporate strategy and business organization

	Tending towards decentralization	*Tending towards centralization*
Business activities	Diversified	Single/integrated
How has the company grown?	By merger/acquisition	Organically
Is the production integrated between plants/companies?	No/little	Yes, a lot
Future strategy	Aggressive growth	Defensive/maintain market share
Accounting	Decentralized local profit centres	Centralized
Marketing	Business unit responsibility, many brand names, no corporate logo	Strong corporate function/unified brand image, logo
Product markets	Varied, numerous, complex	Single, unified
Technical change	Locally designed, highly variable	Centrally designed, integrated systems

Labour markets *contd.*

Are skills unique to the company?	No, most employees are recruited on the basis of previous training/skill attainment	Yes, most employees need significant company-provided training
Who do employees compare themselves with?	Other workers in the community	Other employees in the company

Industrial relations factors
(*NB many of these factors will need to be changed with bargaining realignment*)

	Tending towards decentralization	*Tending towards centralization*
Is the same union recognized throughout the company?	No, wide variety in recognition practices	Yes
Does the main union have a significant percentage of its members in the company?	No, unions are mainly general	Yes, it is an industrial/company union

	Tending towards decentralization	Tending towards centralization
Corporate culture	Weak, performance-based	Strong, unified
How much discretion is traditionally given to local managers?	Considerable	Only a little
Management careers	Matrix, performance-based, business unit responsibility	Functionally organized, centrally directed
Labour markets		
What is the market for key labour?	Local	National
Are there significant variations in local labour market conditions?	Yes	No
How dispersed are sites, business units?	Geographically dispersed	Concentrated
Are internal labour markets a common feature in the company?	For only a few senior managers	Yes, for most grades of employee
Does the main union have a tradition of head office control?	No, dispersed full-time officers	Yes, head office based full-time officers
Who does the company prefer to bargain with?	Shop steward, lay officials	National full-time officers
Is there a tradition of shop steward combined committees?	No, weak or non-existent	Yes, they are well organized
Past policy on information disclosure for collective bargaining	Restricted to local issues	Centrally controlled, local profit figures not provided
Past arrangements for bargaining in the company	Some local bargaining and bonuses, local rates	Exclusively at corporate level
Consultative committees	Well-developed at local levels	Only at corporate level
Is there a history of interplant pay comparisons and co-ordinated industrial action?	No	Yes
Where is the final stage of internal disputes procedures?	Local level	Corporate/major division level

Table 7.5 Decentralization planning checklist (continued)

Industrial relations factors (NB many of these factors will need to be changed with bargaining realignment)	Tending towards decentralization	Tending towards centralization
Do fringe benefits and conditions of service vary between units?	Yes	No, common standards apply
Are there wide variations in actual earnings and hours of work between units?	Yes	No, standard pay rates and hours of work apply
Payment systems	Numerous and complex	Simple/unified
Job evaluation	Locally based in business units	Company-wide

Industrial relations factors *contd.*		
Are there wide variations in labour productivity between plants or areas?	Yes	No
Is there a perceived need for bonuses or incentive payments?	Yes	No
Is the corporate or major division personnel department well-staffed?	No	Yes
Negotiating skills	Diffused and widespread	Concentrated

Source: Purcell, J., 'How to manage decentralised bargaining', *Personnel Management*, 1989.

Furthermore, even where bargaining has been decentralized, this does not mean that local managers are given a completely free hand as to how they conduct negotiations. In fact, rather the opposite appears to be true. Thus, one study of 175 large multi-establishment enterprises found that two-thirds of those with establishment-bargaining had a central policy on pay settlements or issued pay guidelines, and a similar proportion indicated that there were consultations with management at higher levels before the start of negotiations.[34] Overall, only 17 per cent of the establishments surveyed reported that there were no such higher-level policies, guidelines or consultation.

Nature of agreements

The provisions of collective agreements may remain in force for varying lengths of time, ranging from a few weeks to several years, depending on the subjects covered. Negotiations over pay typically take place annually, but do not always. For example, a number of companies have, in recent years, preferred to negotiate longer-term deals as a way of creating a more predictable and stable employee relations environment. Such agreements, which generally still provide for annual increases, usually last either two or three years.

Collective agreements in Britain are, with a few exceptions, not legally binding on the signatories, although some of their terms may be incorporated into employees' individual contracts of employment. They also tend to be relatively insubstantial and imprecise when compared with those in the more legally based industrial relations systems, such as those in North America.

Indeed, it has been noted frequently that the British system of industrial relations embodies a relatively high degree of informality compared with other industrialized countries. The extent of this informality was, in fact, a central theme of the 1968 report of the Royal Commission on Trade Unions and Employers' Associations.[35] Known as the Donovan Commission, after the Commission's chairman Lord Donovan, this criticized the degree of reliance then placed on informal understandings and agreements, on the grounds that they were a major source of disorder in periods of high unemployment and rapid change because of the misunderstandings, inconsistencies and comparability-based claims they could give rise to. The Commission consequently went on to recommend that companies should develop comprehensive and authoritative collective bargaining machinery at the company and/or work-place level.

The period since Donovan has undoubtedly seen a considerable increase in the formality of many aspects of employer–union relationships. Most medium and large work-places, for example, now have formal procedures covering union recognition and the handling of grievances and disputes (see Chapter 9). The growth in trade-union membership and influence during the 1970s, as well as the recommendations of the Donovan Commission, were both important factors in encouraging this growth. Other important influences were the various statutory employment rights introduced during this period and the need these generated for companies to develop clear and consistent policies in response to them. This is true, for example, of the statutory provisions on unfair dismissal, race and sex discrimination, equal pay, and time off for union officials to undergo training and carry out their duties.[36]

Nevertheless, care must be taken not to exaggerate the extent to which industrial relations in Britain are now formalized. Informal understandings and agreements still continue to be concluded by local union representatives and managers, although less commonly than at the time of the Donovan report. In addition, many agreements continue to incorporate a substantial degree of imprecision. In part, this imprecision reflects the types of fudges that sometimes have to be made to resolve disagreements and secure agreement. However, a more important explanation is the desire on the part of one or both sides to retain a degree of flexibility which can possibly be exploited at a later date.[37] Employers, for example, may choose not to concede formally rights and facilities they have given to shop stewards on an informal basis, on the grounds that they can be more easily withdrawn and less easily used to secure yet further concessions. Similarly, they may avoid detailing in too great a detail the duties of particular types of workers, so as to enable these to be interpreted more liberally at a later date. For their part, union representatives may seek to leave certain types of concession vague, so that they have the opportunity to try to minimize their real significance through later discussions with local managers about how they are to be applied.

These last points serve to highlight how the provisions of collective agreements, and particularly those dealing with work duties, are capable of being interpreted in very different ways by the signatories, in response to changes in the internal and external environment and shifts in the balance of power between them. In turn, this latter point means that calculations about the potential advantages and disadvantages of informality are likely to change. The content of flexibility and productivity agreements, that is agreements under which unions concede changes in working practices and other matters in return for improvements in terms and conditions, illustrate this. Thus in the 1960s and 1970s trade-union representatives, against a background of growing membership and strength, frequently sought to include only general statements about the way job demarcations were to be broken down, as this provided them with the potential opportunity to claw back the concessions made through subsequent local discussions. Employers, on the other hand, were often far keener to spell out precisely what changes were required. Over the past decade, however, there has been a marked tendency for employers to favour the former approach because of their confidence that broad general statements of intent can be made to deliver.

References

1. Pelling, H., *A History of British Trade Unionism* (5th edn), London: Macmillan, 1992.
2. See Kelly, J. and Bailey, R., 'British trade union membership density and decline in the 1980s: a research note', *Industrial Relations Journal*, 20(1), 1989, pp. 54–61; and Beaston, M. and Butcher, S., 'Union density across the employed workforce', *Employment Gazette*, 1993, pp. 673–89.
3. Bain, G. S. and Price, R., 'Union growth: dimensions, determinants and destinies', in *Industrial Relations in Britain*, ed. Bain, G. S., Oxford: Blackwell, 1983.
4. Bird, D., Kirosingh, M., and Stevens, M., 'Membership of trade unions in 1990', *Employment Gazette*, April 1992, pp. 185–90.
5. Beaston and Butcher, *Employment Gazette*, pp. 673–89.
6. Towers, B., 'Running the gauntlet: British trade unions under Thatcher, 1979–88', *Industrial and Labor Relations Review*, 42(2), 1989, pp. 163–88.
7. Bain and Price, *Industrial Relations in Britain*.
8. Undy, R., Ellis, V., McCarthy, W. E. J. and Halmos, A. M., 'The role of union leadership in membership growth: further criticisms of Bain's theory', in *Trade Unions* (2nd edn), ed. McCarthy, W. E. J., London: Penguin, 1985.
9. Willman, P., 'The logic of "market-share" trade unionism: is membership decline inevitable?', *Industrial Relations Journal*, 20(3), 1989, pp. 260–70.
10. Mason, B. and Bain, P., 'Trade union recruitment strategies: facing the 1990s', *Industrial Relations Journal*, 22(1), 1990.
11. Bird *et al.*, *Employment Gazette*, pp. 185–90.

12. Hyman, R., *Industrial Relations: A Marxist introduction*, London: Macmillan, 1975.
13. Undy, R., Ellis, V., McCarthy, W. E. J. and Halmos, A. M., 'Recent merger movements and future union structure', in *Trade Unions* (2nd edn), ed. McCarthy, W. E. J., London: Penguin, 1985.
14. Trade Union Reform and Employment Rights Act 1993; and James, P., 'Bridlington: a suitable case for treatment?', *Industrial Relations Review and Report*, September 1992, pp. 6–11.
15. S.46 Trade Union and Labour Relations (Consolidation) Act 1992.
16. Michels, R., *Political Parties*, New York: Hearst's, 1915.
17. Hemmingway, J., *Conflict and Democracy*, Oxford: Oxford University Press, 1978.
18. See McIlroy, J., 'The permanent revolution: Conservative law and the trade unions', *Spokesman*, 1991.
19. *ibid*.
20. See, for example, Martin, R., Fosh, P., Morris, H., Smith, P. and Undy, R., 'The decollectivisation of trade unionism? Ballots and collective bargaining in the 1980s', *Industrial Relations Journal*, **22**(3), 1991, pp. 197–208.
21. Beaston and Butcher, *Employment Gazette*, pp. 673–89.
22. Millward, N., Stevens, M., Smart, D. and Hawes, W. R., *Workplace Industrial Relations in Transition: The ED/ESRC/PSI/ACAS surveys*, Aldershot: Gower, 1992.
23. Bain and Price, *Industrial Relations in Britain*, pp. 3–33.
24. Nolan, P., 'Trade unions and productivity: issues, evidence and prospects', *Employee Relations*, **14**(6), 1992, pp. 3–19.
25. Claydon, T., 'Union derecognition in Britain in the 1980s', *British Journal of Industrial Relations*, **27**(2), 1989, pp. 214–24.
26. Batstone, E., Boraston, I. and Frenkel, S., *Shop Stewards in Action*, Oxford: Blackwell, 1977.
27. S.46 Trade Union and Labour Relations (Consolidation) Act 1992.
28. Millward *et al.*, *Workplace Industrial Relations in Transition: the ED/ESRC/PSI/ACAS surveys*.
29. Brewster, C. and Connock, S., *Industrial Relations: Cost-effective strategies*, London: Hutchinson, 1985.
30. 'Decentralised bargaining in practice 1', *Industrial Relations Review and Report*, December 1989, pp. 5–10.
31. See Griffiths, W., 'Kent County Council: a case of local pay determination', *Human Resource Management Journal*, **1**(1), 1990, pp. 100–7.
32. Purcell, J., 'How to manage decentralised bargaining', *Personnel Management*, May 1989.
33. Marginson, P., Edwards, P. K., Martin, R., Purcell, J. and Sisson, K., *Beyond the Workplace: Managing industrial relations in the multi-establishment enterprise*, Oxford: Blackwell, 1988.
34. *ibid*.
35. *Royal Commission on Trade Unions and Employers' Associations*, London: HMSO, 1968.

36. For a succinct review of these provisions see Lewis, D., *Essentials of Employment Law* (3rd edn), London: IPM, 1990.
37. McCarthy, W. E. J., *The role of shop stewards in British industrial relations*, Royal Commission Research Paper No. 1, London: HMSO, 1966.

8

Employee participation

The subject of employee participation has been of long-standing interest to industrial relations researchers and practitioners. Its use receives widespread support from unions, employers and each of the main political parties. Less agreement exists, however, as to the forms it should take and the impact that it has on management–worker relations and organizational performance more generally.

This chapter initially examines what is meant by the term and the different types of arrangements it encompasses. Current developments in the area are then reviewed. Finally, the rationales underlying its use are examined, together with the evidence relating to the validity of these rationales.

What is participation?

A vast literature exists on the subject of employee participation and such related concepts as employee involvement and industrial democracy. Yet there are no universally accepted definitions of what the term means. Indeed, the number of different definitions put forward moved two authors to conclude that 'workers' participation is an old persistent idea with many meanings'.[1] What is clear is that the types of arrangements often included under its umbrella exhibit marked differences in terms of the degree of influence they provide to workers; the form of worker involvement they embody; the level at which they operate and the subject matter covered.

Degree of influence

Organizational decision-making can be viewed along a continuum ranging from total management control at one end to worker domination at the other.[2] In between these two extremes a variety of different levels of involvement can be distinguished, the most common distinctions being: downward communication from management; bilateral or two-way systems of communication, such as information meetings or briefing groups; consultation arrangements whereby employees are given an opportunity to discuss particular issues, while management retains the actual right of decision-making; systems of delegated control, such as job enrichment and autonomous work groups; and various forms of joint decision-making. Worker directors, collective bargaining and the legally based work-council arrangements found in some European countries provide examples of the latter.

The issue of worker influence has been fundamental to the definitional debates over the meaning of employee participation. Thus these have generally centred on the related issues of whether the term should be restricted to arrangements that enable workers potentially to exercise a degree of influence over management questions have been central to discussions about these issues. First, should the term extend to cover management techniques aimed at keeping workers informed or persuading them to accept particular decisions – referred to as 'pseudo participation'?[3] Secondly, should it be restricted to arrangements that enable workers to exert control as opposed to mere influence over management?

Form of involvement

Three different types of involvement can be distinguished: direct or individual; indirect or representative; and financial. Suggestion schemes, quality circles and briefing groups are among the practices falling within the first of these categories. Worker directors, collective bargaining and joint consultative committees are examples of those falling within the second. The third form of participation covers schemes that provide workers with an ownership stake in their organization and/or establish some direct link between their earnings and the organization's financial performance. It therefore encompasses share-option and profit-sharing schemes, as well as various types of incentive payment system (see Chapter 4).

Level and subject matter of participation

Participative arrangements can operate at a number of different levels within an employing organization. In multisite enterprises, for example, five main levels can be distinguished: the work task; the department/section; the establishment; the division/region; and the whole organization. Similarly, the range of subjects covered by participative arrangements can vary. At one extreme the matters discussed could include issues of strategic importance to the whole enterprise, such as product range, investment decisions and other commercial and financial matters of similar significance. At the other, the subject matter may be more restricted to issues relating to items quite peripheral to the running of the business, for example the state of the car park or the canteen. Between these two extremes are issues of varying degrees of operational importance, such as those concerned with production or service decisions.[4]

Clearly the level at which participation operates and the subject matter encompassed by it are closely related. An alternative approach to classifying participation by level is therefore to conflate these two factors and in this way overcome the difficulties of producing a list of physical levels that is applicable to all organizations. Writers adopting this approach have, for example, drawn a distinction between local, medium and distant participation.[5] Briefly, local participation is seen to involve decision-making of immediate relevance to the worker's job, which is characteristically made by them, their supervisors or first-line managers. The broad range of decision-making activities that traditionally fall within the authority of middle managers forms the focus of medium participation, while the distant form concerns arrangements that operate at the highest levels of the organizational hierarchy.

Main forms of participation

In the above discussion reference was made to various different types of participative arrangements. We go on to outline some of the most common of these, other than collective bargaining which is dealt with in the next chapter, and task-based systems of participation, which are covered in Chapter 5. However, before doing so it must be stressed that the use made of them in Britain is, for the most part, dependent on the voluntary actions of employers and unions since, outside the area of occupational health and safety (see Chapter 6), no general legal obligations are imposed on employers regarding the creation of institutions for work-force participation – a situation that contrasts with the position in most other member states of the European Community.[6] However, companies employing more than 250 people are obliged to detail in their annual reports the actions they have taken during the previous financial year to introduce, maintain or develop employee involvement.[7]

Communication methods

Many different methods are used by employers to provide information to workers. They include house journals, notice-boards, videos, team briefings, employee reports, attitude surveys and suggestion schemes. These different schemes can be divided broadly into two categories: those essentially involving the provision of information from employers to workers – often labelled 'downward' systems; and those involving some active participation on the part of workers. The latter can, in turn, be subdivided into those that primarily require information to be passed from workers to employers (such as suggestion schemes) and those that provide for some degree of interaction between workers and members of management/supervision.

Historically, employers have made the greatest use of the passive forms of downward and upward communication. However, recent years have seen a growing number of organizations utilizing more interactive methods as a means of ensuring that information is both received and understood by employees. Systems of team briefing have provided the main means by which this interaction has been encouraged.

Team briefing – a system strongly advocated by the Industrial Society – provides a method by which top management can cascade information through the organization. Under it each tier of management holds meetings of around half an hour's duration, with small groups of between four and twenty subordinates. The information provided at these meetings typically consists of 70 per cent local news of immediate relevance to the employees concerned, with the remainder comprising more general information about developments in the organization as a whole. During the meetings workers are given the opportunity to ask questions and make comments on the information provided.

Problem-solving groups

As their name implies, problem-solving groups involve employees being brought together to discuss, and hopefully resolve, operational problems related to their work. Such groups may be formed to carry out a one-off project or else be established on a more permanent basis, possibly as part of total-quality management systems. Where the latter is the case, they are frequently referred to as quality circles, although some organizations have chosen to give them other titles, such as zone circles and job improvement committees. Such titles often provide a more accurate description of the activities of groups since, in most cases, their remit extends beyond issues relating to product or service quality to encompass more general efficiency questions.

Quality circles were first used on a large scale in Japan, although the concept originated in the United States. They have been used in Britain since the end of the 1970s. Circles typically consist of between four and a dozen volunteers who meet under the guidance of a group leader – usually, but not always, a supervisor. Participation is normally on a voluntary basis and the work of circles is usually supported by a facilitator who is intended to act as a source of information and advice, and as a liaison between individual circles and the rest of the organization.

The length and frequency of circle meetings vary, depending on the circumstances. In some organizations they meet weekly for half an hour or an hour. In others they meet for an hour every fortnight or for between two and three hours each month. Circle members generally receive training in interpersonal skills and a range of analytical techniques such as brainstorming, Pareto analysis, action planning and statistical process control.

Share ownership/profit sharing

Three main types of scheme can be distinguished under this heading: share options, cash-based profit sharing and share-based profit sharing. Each of these types can, in turn, be subdivided according to whether they are Inland Revenue approved, and hence provide various tax benefits, or not, with the result that six different

Table 8.1 Types of financial participation

Scheme type	Availability	Legislation	Tax concessions
Cash-based profit sharing	Usually all employees	Not applicable	None
Profit-related pay (PRP)	At least 80% of relevant	1987 Finance Act	PRP exempt from tax (PAYE)
Immediate (unrestricted) share scheme	Usually all	Not applicable	None
Inland Revenue approved deferred share trust (ADST)	All employees with 5 years' service – others if invited	1978 Finance Act	Exempt from tax (PAYE) if held for 5 years
Mixture of share and cash schemes	Usually all employees	1978 Finance Act	ADST part exempt as above
Company-wide share-option schemes	All employees, often at the directors discretion	Not applicable	None
Executive share option (discretionary)	Selected executives	1984 Finance Act	Exempt from tax (PAYE) if exercised between 3 and 10 years from date of grant
Company-wide savings-related share-option schemes (SAYE)	All employees with 5 years' service, others if invited	1980 Finance Act	Exempt from tax (PAYE)

Source: Adapted from Baddon, L. *et al.*, *Developments in profit-sharing and employee share ownership*, Centre for Research into Industrial Democracy and Participation, University of Glasgow, June 1987.

forms of scheme can be distinguished. Details of these are given in Table 8.1. In many cases organizations make use of a variety of them.

Profit sharing has been utilized by employers for more than 100 years, but the scale of its use has varied during this period. Recent years have seen an upsurge in interest, primarily as a result of the tax incentives provided under the Finance Acts 1978, 1980, 1984 and 1987. The determination of how much is to be distributed under such schemes varies. Some companies employ a fixed formula, the complexity of which can range, in the case of approved deferred share trust (ADST) and unapproved cash schemes, from simple fixed percentages of profits to the use of complex added value methods. Others leave the matter to the discretion of directors. In general, however, the proportion of profits distributed under such schemes is small, typically around 3 per cent.[8]

Different approaches are also used with regard to how the total profit share is to be distributed among individual employees – subject to the requirement in approved schemes that the method used applies to all relevant employees. The most common approach is to distribute profit shares on the basis of current pay levels, but job grade, service or a combination of service and pay are sometimes used. A small number of companies make payments of equal value to all employees.

Worker directors

In a number of European countries legislation exists requiring representatives of workers to be appointed to the boards of certain types of companies. The balance between employee and shareholder representatives differs under these schemes, the most advanced arrangements providing for equal representation. In some countries where such representation is legally required, a two-tier board structure exists comprising supervisory and management boards. Where this is the case, worker representation is often restricted to the first of these bodies.

Little use has been made of worker directors by British companies. However, such directors existed in British Steel for a number of years following the nationalization of the steel industry in 1965 and for a two-year period from 1978 to 1980 in the Post Office. The latter scheme was introduced following the 1977 report of a committee of inquiry on board-level representation, chaired by Lord Bullock.

The Bullock committee had been set up by the then Labour government against a background of growing interest in the possible value of board-level representation. This interest stemmed from two main forces. First, a belief in some parts of the union movement that worker directors could provide a means of increasing the depth of participation beyond the issues normally covered by collective bargaining. Secondly, the proposal in the EC's draft fifth directive on company law that the appointment of worker directors be made mandatory for all companies with over 500 employees.

In its subsequent report the majority of the committee's members recommended that legislation be introduced providing for worker directors to be appointed in all companies with 2000 or more workers.[9] This representation was to be based on a $2X + Y$ formula under which there would be equal numbers of shareholder and worker representatives, supplemented by an uneven number of independent members. This board-level representation was not to be mandatory, but would only have to be introduced if it secured work-force approval in a ballot requested by recognized unions. Controversially, it was proposed that where this approval was obtained, it should be left to the unions to determine who was to be appointed rather than the work-force as a whole – the so-called single channel of representation.

The Bullock committee's recommendations were greeted with hostility from employers and were also opposed by parts of the union movement. A White Paper putting forward rather weaker measures was eventually published, but nothing came of this as the Labour government lost office in 1979.[10] Whether a future government decides to consider the issue of board-level representation again remains to be seen. It is clear that there will be no impetus as a result of European pressures, since present EC proposals on worker participation would not, if adopted, force the United Kingdom to introduce legislation relating to worker directors.[11]

Joint consultation

Joint consultation is a process through which managers and representatives meet on a regular basis to exchange views and discuss matters of mutual interest. Traditionally, joint consultation has been distinguished from collective bargaining on the grounds that, unlike the latter, it leaves ultimate decision-making power with employers, rather than providing for a degree of power sharing. In practice, however, this distinction, particularly in strongly unionized workplaces, blurs, and a degree of negotiation may take place in committee meetings.

Unionized work groups will usually be represented on committees by shop stewards. Where a committee covers both union and non-union groups, then the representatives of the latter will normally be appointed through some form of election process. Some organizations have different committees covering non-manual and manual staff, while multisite enterprises also frequently operate committees at both the work-place and wider-organizational levels. Production, pay and employment issues, health and safety, and working practices and work organization are the topics most commonly discussed at meetings.

The relationship that exists between joint consultation, on the one hand, and collective bargaining, on the other, is one that has attracted considerable attention. In the 1960s a common view was that joint consultation would decline as trade-union power and organization increased.[12] Evidence from the 1970s, however, suggests that the reverse actually happened. This development prompted a number of researchers to examine more closely the nature of the link between the processes of consultation and bargaining. This research has shown that the nature of the relationship existing between these two processes varies considerably between organizations. Two main models have been distinguished, the competitive and the adjunct.[13]

As its name implies, the competitive model is used to describe situations where joint consultation and collective bargaining are viewed as competing models of involvement. In other words, the type of situation underlying the 1960s view of the relationship between the two processes. Under this model consultation is essentially seen by management as a means of keeping some issues away from the negotiating-table and of moderating the views of shop stewards and their members. In some cases the pursuance of these objectives may involve divorcing worker representation on consultative committees from the work-place union organization and hence creating two parallel channels of representation.

In contrast, under the alternative adjunct model, collective bargaining and joint consultation are viewed as two mutually supporting activities. Here consultation is seen as providing a valuable forum through which some types of issues can be discussed in a less conflictual and more problem-solving environment. More specific attractions include its value as a means of sounding out the other party's views prior to the commencement of formal negotiations, creating a greater degree of trust between the two sides, and providing a useful training-ground for less experienced management and trade-union representatives.

The relative importance of these two models appears to have varied from one period to another in response to changes in the economic and political environment confronting organizations. The growth of consultation in the 1970s against a background of union strength seems, for example, to have reflected a belief on the part of both management and unions about the positive contribution it could make to the maintenance of satisfactory relationships between them. Its continued widespread use in the 1980s, however, has partly reflected employer attempts to use it as a means of limiting the range of issues that are the subject of collective negotiations with unions.

Some of the single-union deals concluded on greenfield sites, notably with Japanese companies, illustrate this point. Thus, a central feature of a number of these has been the establishment of what are frequently called company councils, the employee side of which are work-force elected rather than trade-union appointed, although one or more seats may be reserved for union representatives. In most cases these councils are very similar to traditional consultative committees. However, the role of a small number also extends to discussions about adjustments to terms and conditions of employment. They therefore effectively marginalize union involvement over such adjustments unless the council is unable to resolve them.[14]

The creation of elected bodies of this type in unionized work-places has prompted employers in more traditional environments to consider their establishment. This process of reappraisal is being further encouraged by current EC proposals on worker consultation. At present there are three main sets of proposals at various stages of discussion within the EC: the draft European Company Statute, the revised draft fifth directive on company law and the draft works council directive.[15] At present each of these cannot proceed because of opposition from the UK government. The crucial point about them for present purposes, however, is that the first two appear to preclude the use of non-elective forms of worker representation. Their eventual adoption would therefore seem likely to further encourage the establishment of consultative forums not directly based on trade-union organization.

Trends and rationales

More generally, the distinction between the adjunct and competitive models of joint consultation raises the issue of the motives underlying employer initiatives to encourage employee participation. Therefore, attention now turns to this issue. More specifically, this section examines the different objectives underlying such initiatives and the contribution they make to explaining recent developments in the area. The next section goes on to consider the extent to which these objectives are achieved and the factors that influence the degree of their achievement.

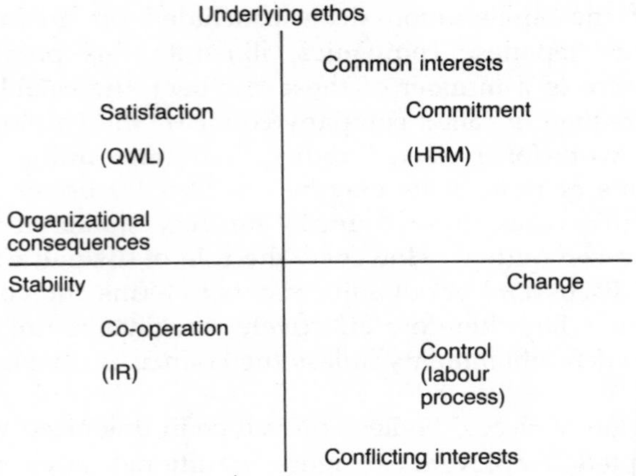

```
                        Underlying ethos

                            Common interests

         Satisfaction              Commitment

           (QWL)                     (HRM)


    Organizational
    consequences

  Stability                                 Change

         Co-operation
                                   Control
           (IR)                    (labour
                                   process)


                            Conflicting interests
```

Source: Marchington, M. *et al.*, *New Developments in Employee Involvement*, Employment Department Research Paper No. 2, London: HMSO.

Figure 8.1 Perspectives underlying the introduction of participatory
arrangements

Objectives

In a recent study the authors analyzed the differing perspectives
underlying the introduction of participatory arrangements along two
dimensions: the ethos underlying them, assessed in terms of the
degree to which they are seen to embody common or conflicting
interests between management and the work-force; and whether
they are intended to contribute to greater organizational stability, on
the one hand, or change, on the other.[16] On the basis of this
analysis, the authors distinguished between participative arrangements in terms of whether they aim to increase worker satisfaction,
commitment, employer–worker co-operation or management control
(see Figure 8.1).

Each of these potential objectives has undoubtedly informed
employer policies with regard to employee participation over the
years. However, their relative importance in explaining trends in the
area has been the subject of considerable debate.

Traditionally, two main explanations have been put forward to
explain historical shifts in the use made of participative
arrangements.[17] The first, the cyclical model, is rooted in Marxist
analysis. It is based on the view that employer interest in such
arrangements waxes and wanes cyclically according to how far their

authority and legitimacy are seen to be challenged by workers and their trade unions. When worker power is high, it is argued that employers resort to employee participation as a means of heading off potential damage to their control. When it falls this interest recedes.

The second main historical analysis, the evolutionist, is almost opposite to the cyclical model. According to this, there is a long-term shift towards greater democracy in capitalist economies as a result of a range of economic and labour-force developments which make more authoritarian styles of management less tenable. These developments are seen to include the increased technical complexity of modern work processes, the presence of a more educated and aspirant work-force and a gradual change in societal values towards greater democracy.

Differing views exist as to the value and validity of these two perspectives, and hence to the extent to which the four objectives listed above have informed historical trends regarding employee participation. Some researchers argue that the available evidence supports the cyclical analysis, others the evolutionist. A third group criticizes both models on the grounds that the universalistic and deterministic assumptions underlying them mean that they are insufficiently sensitive to the way in which economic and political forces impinge on employer decision-making. As a result, it is argued that they are unable adequately to explain variations in the nature and extent of participative developments from one period to another and from one organization to another. Recent trends in the area lend weight to this criticism.

Recent trends and their explanation

The available evidence suggests that since the end of the 1970s employers have introduced a range of measures designed to increase employee participation. The 1980, 1984 and 1990 work-place industrial relations surveys each asked management and union respondents about initiatives taken to increase employee involvement over the previous three or, in the case of the 1984 survey, four years.[18] The proportion of managers responding positively to this question indicates that many organizations, at least outside of private manufacturing, have been adopting such initiatives, and that they have been doing so on an increasing scale. A similar picture emerges with regard to the use of share-option and profit-sharing schemes.

Table 8.2   Recent changes made to increase employee involvement, as reported by managers, by broad sector, 1984 and 1990 (percentages)

	All establishments		Private manufacturing		Private services		Public sector	
	1984[a]	1990[b]	1984	1990	1984	1990	1984	1990
Any initiative	**35**	**45**	**35**	**32**	**33**	**45**	**36**	**55**
New consultative committee	4	4	5	4	2	3	4	3
New health and safety committee	*	*	*	*	–	*	1	*
New joint meetings	5	9	6	5	4	9	6	13
Representative on top governing body	*	1	–	–	*	*	*	2
Any of above	**9**	**13**	**11**	**9**	**6**	**13**	**10**	**18**
Improved existing committee	1	1	1	1	2	*	1	1
More two-way communication	12	13	15	7	12	12	11	19
More information to employees	4	5	6	3	5	5	2	6
Participation scheme	1	*	1	*	1	1	1	*
Share scheme	*	*	1	*	*	1	–	–
Suggestion scheme	*	2	1	2	*	2	*	2
Autonomous work groups	2	2	*	1	2	*	4	4
Management training for participation	1	1	*	1	1	1	1	*
Quality of working life/job satisfaction	*	1	*	1	2	1	–	1
Quality circles	*	2	*	5	2	2	*	*
Involvement in technical change	*	*	*	*	*	*	–	*
Briefing/training groups	1	5	*	6	1	5	1	4
Delegation	3	6	1	2	4	8	3	6
Incentive scheme	1	3	*	1	1	5	1	2
Management reorganization	1	2	*	2	1	2	2	1
Any of above	**25**	**33**	**25**	**24**	**27**	**33**	**24**	**38**
Other answer	2	4	1	2	1	4	3	6
Don't know/not answered	1	*	1	–	*	–	2	*

*Fewer than 0.5 per cent.
[a]1984: in the four years prior to interview.
[b]1990: in the three years prior to interview.
Source: Millward, N. et al., *Workplace Industrial Relations in Transition: The EDIESRCI PSIIACAS surveys*, Aldershot: Gower, 1992.

As to the types of involvement initiatives introduced, Table 8.2 points to the fact that most have been individual based and primarily concerned with the improvement of two-way communications. In contrast, relatively few employers have sought to create new representative committees. Recent research into the employee involvement strategies of twenty-five organizations reveals a similar picture to this and, additionally, gives some insight into the rationales underlying them.[19]

Six broad types of rationale were discovered: informing and educating workers about the business position of the organization; encouraging employees to identify with the company and exercise discretionary skills towards its success; tapping employee knowledge and ideas through upward problem-solving techniques; improving staff recruitment and retention; contributing to conflict handling and organizational stability; and responding to legislative developments in the area of financial participation and 'best practice' in other organizations. Overall, the findings suggest that many of the involvement initiatives adopted over the past decade have been driven by the commitment/satisfaction objective detailed in Figure 8.1. Although, in some cases, the developments involved have resulted in the marginalization of unions, this is generally seen as a by-product – albeit one often viewed positively by managers – rather than a central objective.

The rationales underlying recent participative developments, particularly as they have occurred against a background of high unemployment and diminishing union power and membership, inevitably cast doubt over the value of the cyclical model as a means of explaining them. They also suggest that the initiatives adopted have frequently been driven less by narrow industrial relations considerations than by broader business pressures and demands. At the same time, the emphasis placed on softer, individual forms of involvement, and the growing importance of the competitive model of joint consultation, suggest that the developments taking place do not represent a radical move towards the creation of more democratic employment structures and processes.

Whether, as the evolutionist model would suggest, current initiatives mark a stage in the development of such structures and processes is less clear. The pace of technological and product market changes linked to growing competitive pressures would, at one level, appear to point logically in that direction. However, it is far from certain, in the absence of union, legislative or labour-market pressures, that the majority of employers will voluntarily countenance developments along this line. What can be said with more certainty, as shall be seen below, is that many participative initiatives introduced over the past decade are likely to yield disappointing results for employers in the long term unless they give workers more say over their design and implementation.

Impact of participation

Evaluating the impact of participative initiatives is far from easy, because of the methodological problems of conducting research in the area. Two particular problems characterize much of the research conducted to date. The first of these is the cross-sectional nature of many of the studies, and the uncertainty this gives rise to regarding the long-term effects of the arrangements investigated. The second, and related problem, is the difficulty of isolating the effects of participative arrangements from those of other factors which can affect their operation. For example, the introduction of revised incentive payment schemes, recent redundancies or a deteriorating financial position.

Existing findings on the impact of the employee participation, perhaps not surprisingly, are marked by a considerable degree of uncertainty and inconsistency. A case in point is the alleged link between opportunities to participate and employee satisfaction. Thus, one review of the relevant literature concluded that 'there is hardly a study in the entire literature which fails to demonstrate that satisfaction at work is enhanced or that other generally acknowledged beneficial consequences accrue from a genuine increase in workers' decision-making power'.[20] In contrast, a later review moved the authors to conclude that 'There is little more than a suggestion that immediate participation is a determinant of worker satisfaction, and even less support for this hypothesis at the distant level'.[21]

The evidence available on the impact of participation consists of both attitudinal and quantitative assessments of its effects on such indices of organizational performance as labour turnover, absenteeism, productivity, profitability and conflict at work. On balance, the evidence suggests that participative techniques can have potentially beneficial consequences in each of these areas. However, the extent and nature of these consequences is highly contingent on the types of arrangements introduced, and the way and circumstances in which they are developed and implemented. In other words, participation cannot be viewed as some form of universal panacea for labour-related problems.

The effects of techniques such as team briefing, quality circles and joint consultative committees have been found to be very much influenced by the way in which they are structured, and various sets of prescriptive recommendations exist as to the structural features that are necessary preconditions for their effective operation.[22] In the case of team briefing, for example, the following points have been recommended:

- the central message should be based upon ideas following a senior management or board meeting;
- at each level, the central message should contribute no more than 30 per cent of the total message;
- teams should be based around a common production or service area, rather than an occupation;
- the team should comprise between four and fifteen people;
- meetings should be held at least monthly and on a regular, pre-arranged basis;
- the aim should be to brief all employees within forty-eight hours;
- the meeting should not last more than thirty minutes;
- there should be no more than four levels in the cascade system from senior management to the office or shop floor;
- general discussion should be discouraged;
- time should be left for questions about the brief at the end of the input from the leader;
- the leader should be the manager or supervisor of the section concerned; and
- leaders must be trained in the principles and skills of how to brief.

More generally, participative techniques have been found to be influenced by a wide range of environmental forces. These include the degree of trust that exists between management and the work-force, the degree of support provided by management in terms of both resources and commitment, the amount of real influence they provide to workers, how they fit in with the more general management style, the extent to which employees are involved in their development, and the financial rewards associated with them, either at the stage they are introduced or as a result of their operation. In other words, and at the cost of perhaps slightly oversimplifying the situation, the extent to which participative initiatives achieve their intended objectives is very much dependent on the approach adopted to their development and operation, and the degree of fit that exists between them and the organization's more general approach to human resource management.

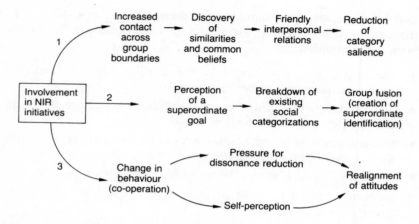

Source: Kelly, J. and Kelly, C., 'Them and us: social psychology and the new industrial relations', *British Journal of Industrial Relations*, **29**(1), 1991, pp. 25–48.

Figure 8.2   Three possible routes to attitude change

A recent analysis of the psychological literature on attitude change and its relevance to participative initiatives reinforces this point.[23] In this it is noted that attitude change can be secured through three main channels (see Figure 8.2): first, through increasing contact between superiors and subordinates; secondly, by creating super-ordinate goals – an important objective presumably underlying the wide use currently being made of mission statements; and, thirdly, by encouraging changes in behaviour which subsequently prompt employees to reappraise their existing attitudes and seek to bring them into line with the relevant behaviour. Each of these routes is noted to be dependent on one or more necessary conditions being present. First, employees having some say in the setting up of schemes and whether they participate in them. Secondly, whether workers trust managers with regard to what they say and their ability to take the appropriate actions. Thirdly, the extent to which there is equality of status and outcomes in the operation of the participatory arrangements and in the employment relationships as a whole. Finally, the degree of institutional support provided.

One final point that merits mention in relation to the factors conducive to successful participation is the relationship that exists between individual and collective forms. Some North American evidence on this suggests that employee participation is most likely to be successful where these two forms of participation occur simultaneously and in a mutually supportive way. In particular, the research suggests that individual-level initiatives adopted without support from any worker representative systems present may meet work-force resistance and hence not achieve management objectives. The introduction of such techniques without this support can, in turn, serve to damage the operation of the representative systems.[24]

Some British experience lends weight to this view. Unions are often suspicious of individual participative techniques, because they fear that they will serve to marginalize their position – a fear that has, as already noted, been borne out in some cases. Consequently, unions have opposed such initiatives in some organizations. Indeed, in some cases they have succeeded in either stopping the introduction of such initiatives or significantly harming their implementation. These experiences and the American evidence referred to above therefore suggest that employers should seek, as far as possible, to obtain union support for initiatives aimed at securing greater employee involvement at the individual level, in order to minimize a potentially damaging conflict between the two channels of participation.

References

1. Walker, K. and Greyfre de Bellecombe, L., 'Worker participation: the concept and its implementation', *International Institute of Labour Studies Bulletin*, **2**, 1967.
2. See Blumberg, P., *Industrial Democracy: The sociology of participation*, London: Constable, 1968; Guest, D., 'A framework for participation', in *Putting Participation into Practice*, eds Guest, D. and Knight, K., Aldershot: Gower, 1979.
3. Pateman, C., *Participation and Democratic Theory*, Cambridge: Cambridge University Press, 1970.
4. Marchington, M., Goodman, J., Wilkinson, A. and Ackers, P., *New Developments in Employee Involvement*, Employment Department Research Paper No. 2, London: Employment Department, 1992.
5. Wall, T. and Lisheron, J., *Workers' Participation: A critique of the literature and some fresh evidence*, London: McGraw-Hill, 1977.
6. *Employee participation in Europe*, European Industrial Relations Review, Report No. 4, London: Industrial Relations Services, 1990.
7. S.1 Employment Act 1982. Statutory obligations also exist with regard to work-force consultation over redundancies and the transfer of an undertaking. See s.99 Trade Union and Labour Relations (Consolidation) Act 1992, and s. *Transfer of Undertakings (Protection of Employment) Regulations 1981*.

8. Smith, G., 'Profit sharing and employee share ownership in Britain', *Employment Gazette*, 1986.
9. *Report of the Committee of Inquiry on Industrial Democracy (Bullock Report)*, Cmnd 6706, London: HMSO, 1977.
10. *Industrial democracy*, Cmnd 2358. London: HMSO, 1978.
11. Hall, M., 'Behind the European Works Council Directive: The European Commission's legislative strategy', *British Journal of Industrial Relations*, **30**(4), 1992, pp. 547–66.
12. McCarthy, W. E. J., *The Role of Shop Stewards in British Industrial Relations*, Research Paper 1, Royal Commission on Trade Unions and Employers' Associations, London: HMSO, 1966.
13. Marchington, M., 'Joint consultation in practice', in *Personnel Management in Britain*, ed. Sisson, K., Oxford: Blackwell, 1989, pp. 378–402.
14. James, P., 'Joint consultation and single union deals', *Industrial Relations Review and Report*, September 1990.
15. Hall, *British Journal of Industrial Relations*, **30**(4), 547–66.
16. Marchington *et al.*, *New Developments in Employee Involvement*.
17. Poole, M., *The Origins of Economic Democracy: Profit sharing and employee shareholding*, London: Routledge.
18. See, for example, Millward, N., Stevens, M., Smart, D. and Hawes, W. R., *Workplace Industrial Relations in Transition: The ED/ESRC/PSI/ACAS surveys*, Aldershot: Gower, 1992.
19. Marchington *et al.*, *New Developments in Employee Involvement*.
20. Blumberg, *Industrial Democracy: The sociology of participation*, p. 123.
21. Wall and Lisheron, *Worker's Participation: A critique of the literature and some fresh evidence*, p. 34.
22. See, for example, Marchington, M., 'Employee participation', in *A Handbook of Industrial Relations Practice*, ed. Towers, B., London: Kogan Page, 1987.
23. Kelly, J. and Kelly, C., 'Them and us: social psychology and the "New industrial relations"', *British Journal of Industrial Relations*, **29**(1), 1991, pp. 25–48.
24. Strauss, G., 'Workers' participation in management', in *Employment Relations*, ed. Hartley, J. and Stephenson, G., Oxford: Blackwell, 1992, p. 310.

9

Conflict and discipline at work

The employment relationship is based on a notion of exchange. Employers provide workers with various rewards, both intrinsic and extrinsic (see Chapter 4), and in return they are expected to carry out the duties assigned to them in a conscientious and efficient way. Both parts of this exchange can give rise to conflict. The same is true of the balance between the two elements. What management may, for example, consider a reasonable reward package may be viewed very differently by workers. Differences of opinion can similarly arise in relation to what constitutes a 'fair day's work' and, more generally, over what represents a reasonable balance between rewards on the one hand and effort on the other.

This chapter commences with an examination of the various manifestations of work-related conflict and a discussion of strike activity and the factors that influence its nature and level. Attention then shifts to the grievance, disputes and disciplinary procedures used by organizations to control and resolve such conflict.

Conflict and its causes

Worker dissatisfaction with their employment situation can exhibit itself in a wide variety of ways. These have commonly been divided into two broad categories: organized and unorganized. The first of these is used to refer to collective forms of conflict which represent attempts on the part of workers to change the conditions deemed unsatisfactory, and encompasses such actions as strikes, go-slows,

171

work-to-rules, overtime bans and even sit-ins and occupations. Unorganized conflict, in contrast, encompasses individual-based forms of behaviour which are less strategically oriented to the achievement of change. Absenteeism, resignations/labour turnover, poor timekeeping, lateness, sabotage and other forms of indiscipline are examples of the types of behaviour included under this heading.

Researchers have suggested that these two broad categories of conflict are interrelated, but different views have been put forward as to the nature of this link. Some have argued that they are positively related – the additive hypothesis – while others have suggested that there is an inverse relationship between them – the alternative hypothesis. The rationale for the first of these is rather unclear, but presumably reflects the view that conflict of all types tends to be influenced by the prevailing industrial relations climate within organizations. The rationale for the second is rather clearer, being that worker dissatisfaction will exhibit itself in one way or another. If the collective avenue is unavailable, then recourse, either consciously or subconsciously, will be made to the individual and unorganized forms.

The evidence to support these hypothesized relationships between organized and unorganized conflict – usually tested in terms of the relationship between absenteeism and strikes – is very mixed.[1] Some studies have found no link between the two at all, others have lent support to the alternative model, while yet others lend weight to the additive one. This lack of consistency in research findings clearly casts doubt on any simple and universal relationship existing between the two forms of conflict. At the same time, it does not follow that they are unrelated in all situations. Rather, the inconsistency of findings is better seen as a reflection of a number of conceptual problems surrounding the distinction between organized and unorganized action.

Behaviour at work occurs within a particular context. The meaning of given types of behaviour cannot therefore be assumed but requires close analysis. The absence of strikes, for example, cannot simply be assumed to indicate harmonious employment relations.[2] It may instead be an indication of workers' sense of vulnerability and powerless *vis-à-vis* their employer. Similarly, such forms of behaviour as labour turnover and absenteeism cannot unquestionably be defined as 'conflict' or unproblematically classified as 'individual'.

Absenteeism can occur for a whole range of reasons, only some of which are work-related.[3] To define it as a measure of conflict is consequently highly questionable. Its relationship with strikes and other forms of collective action is also far less straightforward than is implied in the alternative and additive hypotheses. The coincidence of high absence levels and low strike activity may, for example, reflect collective weakness, as proposed in the alternative hypothesis. It may, however, in other cases reflect a position of collective strength whereby the workforce has managed to secure sufficient control to enable it to gain concessions without overt conflict and allow absence to go largely unpunished by management.[4] In other words, individual and collective forms of conflict may or may not be interrelated and, where they are, the meaning of this relationship can vary from one situation to another.

More generally, the measurement of 'conflict' and hence the degree of harmony present in a work-place is far from easy. Low levels of labour turnover and absenteeism, for example, may indicate the presence of a 'committed' work-force which identifies with employer goals and objectives. On the other hand, they may be more a reflection of recessionary conditions characterized by high unemployment and job security and an accompanying absence of alternative employment. Similar points can, as shall be seen, be made with regard to the explanation of trends in strike action.

Strike patterns

Annual statistics on the number of stoppages, the numbers of workers involved (including those indirectly affected at establishments where stoppages occurred), and working days lost have been compiled by the Employment Department and its predecessors since 1893. These statistics are not comprehensive in two senses. First, they exclude strikes not relating to terms and conditions of employment, and those that last less than a day or involve less than ten workers, unless working days lost total at least one hundred. Secondly, as employers are not obliged to report stoppages falling within the officially recordable category, in practice not all relevant strikes come to the attention of the Employment Department and hence are not recorded.[5]

According to the official statistics, the annual total of stoppages followed a broadly upward trend from the end of the Second World War to the end of the 1970s, although there were marked upward and downward variations within this overall trend. Since 1980 this trend has undergone a dramatic reversal. Thus the figure (369) for 1991 is the lowest since 1933 and can be contrasted with annual averages of 1129 for the 1980s and 2631 for the 1970s.[6] The statistics on working days have, because they are heavily influenced by the occurrence of large disputes, exhibited more variable trends over the post-war period. However, in general terms a similar pattern is discernible: the average annual number of working days lost rose from 3.2 million in 1950–67 to 11.7 million in the period 1968–80, before falling back to below 5 million since 1980.[7] Indeed, the figure of 0.8 million for 1991 was the lowest calendar year total since records began.

In addition to allowing the identification of trends in stoppage numbers and working days lost, the Employment Department's statistics provide information on the industrial distribution of stoppages, and their causes and duration. Up until the 1960s strike action was concentrated in five industry groups – docks, coal-mining, motor vehicles, shipbuilding and iron and steel. Although these industries continue to be relatively strike prone, the late 1960s and 1970s saw their relative importance decline as strike action spread to encompass a far wider range of workers, including such public-sector groups as civil servants, teachers and nurses. This shift in the industrial distribution of stoppages and the associated rise in large public-sector disputes initially coincided with a doubling in the proportion of strikes lasting over five days, this rise reaching a peak in 1979 when 43 per cent of stoppages fell into this category. Since then this increase in the average duration of strikes has not only been reversed, but has been accompanied by a significant rise in the importance of strikes lasting less than a day. Thus nearly 50 per cent of strikes in 1991 were of this duration.

The official statistics classify the causes of strikes into eight categories: wage rates and earnings; extra wages and fringe benefits; duration and pattern of working hours; redundancy issues; trade-union matters; working conditions and supervision; staffing and work allocation; and dismissal and other disciplinary measures. In 1991 the first two of these accounted for 37 per cent of stoppages and 41 per cent of working days lost. The next three most important 'causes' were redundancy (18 and 32 per cent), staffing/work allocation (18 and 8 per cent) and working conditions/supervision (12 and 8 per cent).

The Employment Department's classification of stoppages by cause has been critized for involving a 'misleading simplification' of the factors giving rise to a dispute.[8] First, because it takes no account of the fact that strikes may occur as a result of a combination of different types of grievance. Secondly, because it ignores possible 'latent' sources of conflict which, while important, may be deemed not legitimate or suitable for resolution through the collective bargaining process and hence remain unverbalized.

Data from the 1980, 1984 and 1990 work-place industrial relations survey provide an additional important source of information on the scale, causes and distribution of industrial action.[9] The findings, although not directly comparable with the official statistics on stoppages, broadly confirm the main thrust of the above discussion. Thus they confirm that strike action has fallen over the past decade, they highlight significant variations in strike action between different sectors and show pay issues to be by far the most important reasons given for striking. In addition, the surveys usefully supplement the official statistics by providing data on the extent of non-strike action and the proportion of industrial action made official by unions.

The surveys show that during the first half of the 1980s non-strike action was as frequent as strike action, but that its extent fell far more dramatically than was the case with strikes in the second half of the decade. The rank ordering of the various types of non-strike action remained the same, however, with overtime bans being followed in order of importance by work-to-rules, blacking of work, lock-outs and go-slows (see Table 9.1).

The issue of how far industrial action by union members is made official has been one of long-standing interest. In the 1960s official statistics indicated that 95 per cent of strikes were unofficial in that they had not received official support from the relevant union body, normally the Executive Committee. However, the publication of the relevant figures was eventually stopped on the grounds that they gave a misleading impression of their status *vis-à-vis* the parent union(s). Many strikes, for example, are over before they come to the attention of the national union and, where they subsequently do so, it is not common for them to be made official after the event. To label them as 'unofficial', with the implication that they were unapproved by the unions concerned, is therefore highly questionable. Similarly, the fact that a union chooses not to make a dispute official does not necessarily mean that it disapproves of the action in question. Thus some action may be informally encouraged by full-time officials in order to demonstrate member feelings over an issue and hence strengthen the union negotiating position. In other cases a union may choose not to make a dispute official in order to avoid paying strike benefit or because it is considered impolitic to do so, perhaps because it is in breach of an agreed disputes procedure (see below).

Nevertheless, the work-place industrial relations survey data suggest that in 1990 the majority (65 per cent) of strikes involving manual workers which lasted a day or more were made official, and

Table 9.1   The extent to which establishments were affected by industrial action, as reported by any respondent,[a] 1980, 1984 and 1990 (percentages)

	1980	1984	1990
Strike action	13	19	10
Non-strike action	16	18	5
Strike or non-strike action	22	25	12
Strike action lasting:			
Less than 1 day	6	14	4
1 day or more	9	12	7
1 day but less than a week	–	11	6
1 week or more	–	1	1
Non-strike action:			
Overtime bans/restriction	10	11	3
Work to rule	7	8	2
Blacking of work	5	3	1
Lock-out	1	*	–
Go-slow	1	*	*
Other pressure	1	2	1

*Fewer than 0.5 per cent.
[a]The percentages represent those establishments where either the manager or the manual worker representative or the non-manual worker representative reported industrial action of the type specified.
Source: Millward, N. *et al.*, *Workplace Industrial Relations in Transition: The ED/ESRC/ PSI/ACAS surveys*, Aldershot: Gower, 1992.

that the overwhelming majority (94 per cent) of non-manual ones were similarly supported. These figures must, however, be treated with a degree of caution since they relate to strikes of a day or longer. This omission is likely to be of importance because those of less than a day are perhaps more likely to be of a spontaneous nature, with the result that the proportion of all strikes made official may well be significantly lower.

Explaining strike patterns

The research studies conducted into the causes of strike action exhibit marked differences in terms of both the methodologies adopted and their foci of interests.[10] Case studies have been carried out on particular disputes by both psychologists and sociologists; interindustry and interestablishment variations in strike activity have been examined using official strike statistics and survey data; and longitudinal analyses of strike trends have been conducted by means of time-series models.

A range of explanatory variables have been identified through this body of research. The most important of these can be usefully outlined and discussed under three broad headings: organizational factors; environmental influences; and management–worker attitudes and relationships.

Organizational factors

Cross-sectional analyses of variations in the level of strike action between different work-places have found such action to be positively associated with the presence of payment-by-results schemes, union recognition, shop stewards, multiunionism, the proportion of manual workers who are union members and establishment size. Interindustry studies have found higher than average strike activity to be positively related to a high proportion of large establishments, high earnings levels, labour costs representing a relatively high proportion of total costs, a low proportion of female workers, and a higher degree of ownership concentration. More qualitative studies have further suggested that fragmented patterns of bargaining and the social and physical location of workers play important roles in explaining the strike proneness of particular industries.

This list of explanatory variables is undoubtedly impressive. Unfortunately, little can be said about their relative importance, and the degree of support they receive from the available research is often very mixed. For example, some industries characterized by fluctuating earning and widespread use of piecework have historically had low levels of strike activity and, more generally, not all studies have found an association between such activity and the use of PBR schemes.[11]

Moreover, the meaning of the statistical relationships discovered is often unclear because they are not based on any sound, empirically tested microtheories of work-place behaviour. The reasons for the well-established link between strike action and work-place size, for example, has been explained in a number of ways: economists have explained it in terms of probability theory – the larger the work-place the more interactions between people and hence scope for disagreements, while other theorists have done so in terms of the more bureaucratic and impersonal nature of management in larger plants.

These postulated explanations in turn highlight an even more fundamental problem of statistic-based studies – namely that they represent very partial abstractions from the complex and dynamic reality of work-place industrial relations. Potentially important structural and environmental variables are frequently excluded because of lack of suitable data, while the role of others (e.g. product market conditions) is arguably understated because of data limitations and the cross-sectional methodology adopted, or, as in the case of production technology, because they are inadequately conceptualized and measured. In addition, possible interrelationships between variables are also often not examined in sufficient detail. The same is true of the way in which their influence is mediated by the attitudes of and relationships between managers, workers and trade-union representatives. Yet there seems no reason *per se* why the same variable should have the same effect in different work-places. Indeed the inconsistency of findings referred to suggests that they do not.

Environmental influences

The external economic and political environment can clearly influence the nature of work-place relations. However, the extent and nature of this influence are again difficult to specify precisely.

Econometric studies of variations in strike activity over time have sought to examine the way in which these are correlated with the state of the economy – particular attention being paid to changes in the levels and rate of change of unemployment, prices and wages and the presence and operation of incomes policy. The findings emerging from these studies have been far from satisfactory, since the results obtained vary from study to study and from one time period to another. Moreover, the theoretical rationale for any relationships discovered is frequently open to criticism in much the same way as those emerging from the statistical analysis of interindustry and interestablishment variations in strike action.

Nevertheless, in general, studies do suggest that falling real wages have tended to be associated with higher levels of strike action, while high (or at least rapidly rising) levels of unemployment have the opposite effect. Certainly, the decline in strike action during the 1980s has coincided with historically high levels of unemployment and generally rising levels of real wages. Recent case-study evidence of industrial relations change also bears witness to how worker willingness to make concessions without recourse to industrial action has frequently taken place against a background of falling profits, spare capacity and job losses.[12]

Similarly, there seems little doubt that the broader political environment can influence the nature and scale of industrial conflict, both directly and through, as noted earlier, its influence on union membership growth. The operation of incomes policies, for example, has been found to affect levels of strike action, although the direction of this influence varies. Thus in periods where such policies have received widespread support (or at least compliance) the evidence suggests that they reduce the number of wage-related disputes. In contrast, in periods where policies receive strong resistance, the opposite is the case.

It is not only through incomes policies that the government can influence the level and nature of industrial action. It can also do so through the legal framework relating to the taking of industrial action and, in particular, the scope that this provides for legal action to be taken against unions and strikers.

The British system of industrial relations has frequently been characterized as a voluntaristic one, on the grounds that the law has played a relatively small role in regulating relationships between employers and unions during the twentieth century.[13] Fundamental to this policy of legal abstention was the development of a series of immunities which protected unions from a range of criminal- and civil-law liabilities, such as intimidation and inducing a breach of the employment contract, to which strike action would otherwise make them vulnerable. These immunities, laid down under the Trade Disputes Act 1906, applied to all actions taken in 'contemplation or furtherance of a trade dispute'.

Legislation introduced since 1979 has served to circumscribe severely the scope of these immunities and, in doing so, made unions far more vulnerable to injunctions and actions for damages.[14] For example, the immunities now no longer apply in respect of the following:

1. industrial action which has not received majority support in a secret ballot conducted in accordance with statutory requirements;

2. interunion disputes;

3. picketing conducted away from the work-place of strikers;

4. secondary or sympathetic action;

5. action taken to enforce union membership agreements or the inclusion of membership requirements in commercial contracts; and

6. action not relating 'wholly or mainly' to one of the following matters:

    (a) terms and conditions of employment or the physical conditions in which any workers are required to work;

(b)   engagement or non-engagement, or termination or suspen-
      sion of employment, or the duties of employment of one or
      more workers;
(c)   allocation of work or the duties of employment as between
      workers or groups of workers;
(d)   matters of discipline;
(e)   the membership or non-membership of a trade union on
      the part of workers;
(f)   facilities for officials of trade unions;
(g)   machinery for negotiation or consultation, and other proce-
      dures, relating to any of the foregoing matters, including
      the recognition by employers or employers' associations of
      the right of a trade union to represent workers in any such
      negotiation or consultation or in the carrying out of such
      procedures.[15]

These changes to union immunities have been supplemented by
the introduction of further limitations on the right of those dismissed for taking part in industrial action to complain of unfair
dismissal.[16] Until this time employers could dismiss all those who
had been involved in industrial action and those concerned had no
right of complaint. However, if one or more of the strikers were
re-employed, then the remainder could complain to an industrial
tribunal. This position has now been amended in several important
ways. The effect of which is to restrict the re-employment test to
those particular workers on strike at the time an employee was
dismissed – as opposed to those who had at any time been involved
in the relevant action; enable the selective dismissal of workers
taking part in unofficial action; and allow dismissed strikers to be
re-employed on a selective basis after a three-month time period.

It is difficult to quantify how far these changes in the legal
framework relating to industrial action have contributed to the fall in
strike action since 1979. There seems no doubt, however, that they
have had a significant impact. Certainly, employers have been far
more willing, in a period of trade-union weakness, to take and
threaten legal action than they were under the Industrial Relations
Act 1971 – an earlier and short-lived piece of legislation which also
made unions more vulnerable to legal challenge.

Attitudes and relationships

The differing use made by employers of the legal powers granted
under the legislation introduced over the past decade compared

with those provided under the Industrial Relations Act serves to highlight again the crucial point that institutional and environmental factors do not have any automatic effect on the nature and extent of strike action. Rather, their impact is mediated by the attitudes, objectives and interpretation of employers, workers and union representatives.

In other words, deterministic explanations of behaviour are inadequate to explain the realities of work-place behaviour in general and industrial conflict in particular. This is not to say that such factors are unimportant, since they clearly form the context within which the industrial relations parties act. However, it should be recognized that much day-to-day behaviour is likely to be informed by the attitudes and strategies of the industrial relations parties. A study of a small number of manufacturing plants is of interest in this respect. After investigating a whole range of possible factors that could influence variations in conflict between the plants studied, the authors concluded that: 'Undoubtedly the biggest single factor in the different strike incidence of individual plants, however, emerged as the industry group to which they belonged'. The authors went on to suggest that these industrial variations were 'much more the product of historically acquired attitudes and responses than of "objective" economic or technological conditions.'[17]

Grievance and disputes procedures

The majority of employers have developed procedures to aid the peaceful resolution of management–worker disagreements. Two main types of procedure can be distinguished: grievance and disputes. However, it should be noted that both types of procedures may operate alongside various subject-specific procedures. For example, many organizations operate appeal mechanisms to handle complaints over the results of re-grading and job evaluation exercises.

Although many organizations have separate procedures for handling grievances, on the one hand, and disputes, on the other, it is in practice not always easy to draw a clear distinction between the two types of issue. Typically, they are distinguished on the grounds that the former deals with complaints and queries raised by individual employees, while the latter concerns collective-based matters, normally arising out of negotiations between employers and unions.[18]

However, this distinction is not always easy to apply in practice. Grievances, for example, may be common to a group of workers and hence take on a collective dimension. More generally, unresolved grievances can become the subject of management–union disputes.

The way in which this interface between grievances and disputes is handled varies between organizations. Some organizations maintain completely separate procedures. Others provide for grievances at some stage to be referred to the collective-disputes procedures. Yet others prefer to use just one all-encompassing procedure to handle both grievances and disputes. Where such an approach is adopted, it is normal for provision to be made for collective issues to short-circuit the first stages of the procedure.

Inevitably the precise structure of procedures differs in terms of the number of stages involved in the resolution procedure and the individuals who are involved in them. Multisite organizations may, for example, provide for issues, whether grievances or disputes, to be referred to management personnel outside of a particular location or, alternatively, leave responsibility with local managers. Other employers may be party to disputes procedures forming part of industry-wide agreements, with the result that issues may eventually be handled at a national, industry level.

Nevertheless, it is a common feature of grievance procedures that aggrieved employees initially approach their immediate superior, typically the relevant supervisor (see Figure 9.1). If the matter remains unresolved, then the issue can be raised with the next level of management, for example the departmental manager concerned. In unionized environments it is usually at this stage that an employee's shop steward can get involved. However, practice in this area also differs. Thus, in some cases the steward may be involved from the outset. Indeed a minority of procedures enable stewards initially to raise a grievance on behalf of a member. Moreover, even where this is not the case, this may occur in practice – a point that emphasizes once again the importance of informality in the conduct of industrial relations.

Another way in which procedures vary concerns whether some provision is made for independent third-party intervention. Such intervention can take one of three main forms: conciliation, mediation and arbitration. Conciliation and mediation are closely related. Both involve the use of a third party to provide assistance when internal discussions have reached an impasse. Equally, both leave the internal parties with ultimate responsibility for resolving the issue themselves. The essential difference between them is that a mediator is able to put forward recommendations that are designed

Any grievance or other issues affecting employees must, as a matter of principle, be dealt with as effectively and speedily as possible. Priority should be given to the resolution of any matter by informal means. if this is not possible, the following formal procedure will apply:

Stage 1:   Employee discusses matter with immediate supervisor

Stage 2:   Employee and his representative discuss matter with immediate supervisor and appropriate manager

Stage 3:   Employee and his representative discuss matter with immediate supervisor, appropriate manager and personnel manager.

Note 1:   Stages 1–3 should be completed within a period of 5 working days – any failure to agree will be recorded on a Procedure Report form. The issue will then be referred immediately to the next stage and the manager concerned will be responsible for arranging the next stage meeting.

Stage 4:   The Company Joint Council will deal with issues referred from Stage 3. A meeting will take place within a maximum of ten working days of the Procedure Report being completed or of a request by either party.

Stage 5:   Where an issue arises which requires the attendance and participation of the full-time local official of the union concerned at the Company Joint Council, arrangements may be made to that end.

Stage 6:   If no settlement is reached at Company Joint Council, the dispute will be referred immediately to the Advisory, Conciliation and Arbitration Service (ACAS) for conciliation.

Stage 7:   Failing all other settlement including conciliation, the parties will meet to discuss whether the dispute is to be submitted to arbitration. Whenever arbitration is agreed the following provisions will apply:

    (i)   the arbitrator will be appointed by ACAS.

    (ii)   the terms of reference and the form of arbitration (conventional or pendulum) will be agreed for each case.

    (iii)   the parties to the arbitration will agree to accept and to abide by the award of the arbitrator.

    (iv)   the award of the arbitrator will be legally binding on the company and the unions and will be incorporated (as appropriate) into the respective contracts of employment of the employees of the company.

In the event of an issue arising from a company instruction, the employee will carry out that instruction pending the completion of the procedure provided the instruction is in accordance with statute and safe working practices.

There will be no industrial action of any kind while an issue is in procedure or is the subject of conciliation or arbitration.

Figure 9.1   Grievance procedure

to resolve the matter concerned, while conciliators essentially act as facilitators. By way of contrast, arbitration usually involves the third party making a morally binding award to resolve an issue.

Any form of third-party intervention, by definition, brings an outsider into the internal affairs of an organization. For this reason many employers and union officials are cautious about placing too much reliance on it. This is particularly true of arbitration, where managerial decision-making is effectively usurped by the third party appointed. Against this potential loss of domestic authority has to be set the potential benefits of being able to draw on an outside source of advice and expertise which can view an issue in a more dispassionate manner and perhaps helps avoid the degenerating of an issue into a damaging management–union dispute.

Where procedures do provide for third-party intervention, the nature of this provision and the way in which it is 'triggered' differ considerably. For example, reference may only be made to conciliation or arbitration. Alternatively, it may be provided that these two forms of intervention can be used sequentially.

Three options are available with regard to the triggering of third-party intervention. First, joint reference by the parties to the grievance or dispute. Secondly, unilateral reference by one of the parties. Thirdly, automatic reference whereby a failure to agree internally automatically triggers the referencing of an issue to a third party. Moreover, where more than one form of intervention is provided for in procedures, it may be decided to use differing triggering mechanisms for the different forms. For example, a procedure may provide for joint reference to conciliation followed by unilateral reference to arbitration.

Procedures that provide for automatic recourse to arbitration have been central to recent debates about so-called 'no-strike' deals.[19] This is because, when combined with the normal obligation not to take action in breach of procedure, they effectively preclude a union from calling constitutional industrial action. Optical Fibres, NEK Cables, Bowman Webber, Toshiba, Hitachi and Excel Wound Components are among the companies that have agreements of this type. It must be stressed, however, that unconstitutional action may still occur.

A further issue that arises in relation to arbitration is the question of whether it is to be of the 'conventional' or 'pendulum' type. Under the former, arbitrators are typically given the freedom to come up with compromise awards located somewhere between the final positions of management and union, whereas under the latter they must find for one side or the other. The advantages and disadvantages of pendulum (or, as it is sometimes called, 'last offer' or 'flip-flop') arbitration have received a good deal of discussion in recent years.[20] Advocates emphasize its value in concentrating the minds of the domestic parties on finding their own solution and of avoiding the so-called 'chilling effect' – the process whereby the parties conceal their final negotiating positions so that they have something to 'give' if the issue goes to arbitration. However, critics draw attention to the rather crude nature of the process if a dispute involves a number of distinct topics, and the fact that it precludes arbitrators from formulating awards that take long-term industrial relations considerations into account.

Some large employers, particularly in the public sector, have established their own standing arrangements covering the provision of third-party assistance in dispute resolution. The most common practice is to draw on the services of the Advisory, Conciliation and Arbitration Service (ACAS).

ACAS was established by the government in 1974 and is charged with promoting the improvement of industrial relations.[21] Its work is directed by a council consisting of a chairperson and nine members appointed by the Secretary of State. Three of the members are appointed after consultation with employers' organizations, three after consultation with trade unions and the remainder are independent. Although financed by the state, it cannot by statute 'be subject to directions of any kind from any minister of the Crown as to the manner in which it exercises any of its functions'.

The work of ACAS falls into three main areas: provision of advice; the conducting of inquiries; and the provision of conciliation, mediation and arbitration services. Conciliation and mediation are carried out by the service's own officials, but arbitrators are drawn from a panel of suitably qualified people appointed by the service. In most cases all three processes are carried out by individual ACAS officials or arbitrators. However, ACAS will set up mediation boards on request and will also assist in the creation of specially appointed boards of arbitration, consisting of an ACAS arbitrator and equal numbers of representatives from the employer and union sides to a dispute.

Disciplinary procedures

The 1990 work-place industrial survey found that one or more employees had been dismissed in 41 per cent of work-places with twenty-five or more employees. It further found that 96 per cent of these establishment possessed formal procedures for handling disciplinary and dismissal issues.[22]

The use of formal disciplinary procedures has grown dramatically over the past twenty years. A report produced by the National Joint Advisory Council in the late 1960s, for example, found that just 17 per cent of the 373 firms visited had such procedures, only around half of which were in written form.[23] This expansion in the use of formal procedures has primarily arisen as a result of the advent of statutory provisions on unfair dismissal.

Employees first acquired a right to bring complaints before an industrial tribunal alleging unfair dismissal under the Industrial Relations Act 1971. The relevant statutory provisions, which have been amended in a number of respects since then, are now to be found in the Employment Protection (Consolidation) Act 1978.[24] Section 54 of this statute provides employees with a right not to be unfairly dismissed. However, exclusions and qualifications mean that not all employees are able to bring complaints where this right has been breached. In particular, complaints can only be brought by employees who have two years' continuous service, a figure that increases to five years in the case of those working between eight and sixteen hours a week.

Where a claim of unfair dismissal is brought, it is up to the aggrieved employee to show that a dismissal in law has actually occurred. Once this has been established, it is then up to the employer to show that the reason or principal reason for the dismissal falls within one of the following categories:

- it related to the capability or qualifications of the employee for performing work of the kind that he or she was employed to do;
- it related to the conduct of the employee;
- the employee was redundant;
- the employee could not continue to work in the position held without contravention, either on the employers' part or on that of the employee, of a duty or restriction imposed by statute;
- some other substantial reason of a kind such as to justify the dismissal of an employee holding the position the employee held.

If an employer is unable to convince a tribunal that a dismissal falls into one of these categories, then it will be found to be unfair. If the tribunal is so convinced, then it goes on to consider

> . . . whether in the circumstances (including the size and administrative resources of the employer's undertaking), the employer acted reasonably or unreasonably in treating it as a sufficient reason for dismissing the employee: and that question shall be determined in accordance with equity and the substantial merits of the case.

In considering the reasonableness of an employer's action, a tribunal is required to have regard to the ACAS Code of Practice on Disciplinary Rules and Procedures.[25] Paragraph 10 of this code states that disciplinary procedures should:

1. be in writing;
2. specify to whom they apply;
3. provide for matters to be dealt with speedily;
4. indicate the disciplinary actions that may be taken;
5. specify the levels of management that have the authority to take the various forms of disciplinary action;
6. ensure that immediate superiors do not normally have the power to dismiss without reference to senior management;
7. provide for individuals to be informed of the complaints against them and to be given the opportunity to state their case before decisions are reached;
8. give individuals the right to be accompanied by a trade-union representative or by a fellow employee of their choice;
9. ensure that any investigatory period of suspension is with pay (unless the contract of employment clearly provides otherwise) and specify how pay is to be calculated during such a period;
10. ensure that, except for gross misconduct, no employees are dismissed for a first breach of discipline;
11. ensure that disciplinary action is not taken until the case has been carefully investigated;
12. ensure that individuals are given an explanation for any penalty imposed; and
13. provide a right of appeal and specify the procedures to be followed.

The precise procedural arrangements developed in organizations inevitably vary.[26] In particular, procedures exhibit marked variations with regard to: their coverage (in terms of the organizational level at which they operate, and the workers and subject matter encompassed); the offences and penalties specified; the location of managerial responsibility for taking disciplinary action; how appeals are to be handled; the provision, if any, made for third-party intervention; and arrangements made for employee representation.

A model procedure detailed in the ACAS handbook *Discipline at Work* (see Figure 9.2) provides a useful guide to the more common

1 *Purpose and scope*

This procedure is designed to help and encourage all employees to achieve and maintain standards of conduct, attendance and job performance. The company rules (a copy of which is displayed in the office) and this procedure apply to all employees. The aim is to ensure consistent and fair treatment for all.

2 *Principles*

(a) No disciplinary action will be taken against an employee until the case has been fully investigated.
(b) At every stage in the procedure the employee will be advised of the nature of the complaint against him or her and will be given the opportunity to state his or her case before any decision is made.
(c) At all stages the employee will have the right to be accompanied by a shop steward, employee representative or work colleague during the disciplinary interview.
(d) No employee will be dismissed for a first breach of discipline except in the case of gross misconduct when the penalty will be dismissal without notice or payment in lieu of notice.
(e) An employee will have the right to appeal against any disciplinary penalty imposed.
(f) The procedure may be implemented at any stage if the employee's alleged misconduct warrants such action.

3 *The procedure*

Minor faults will be dealt with informally but where the matter is more serious the following procedure will be used:

Stage 1. Oral warning. If conduct or performance does not meet acceptable standards the employee will normally be given a formal **oral warning**. He or she will be advised of the reason for the warning, that it is the first stage of the disciplinary procedure and of his or her right of appeal. A brief note of the oral warning will be kept but it will be spent after .... months, subject to satisfactory conduct and performance.

Stage 2. Written warning. If the offence is a serious one, or if a further offence occurs, a written warning will be given to the employee by the supervisor. This will give details of the complaint, the improvement required and the time scale. It will warn that action under Stage 3 will be considered if there is no satisfactory improvement and will advise of the right of appeal. A copy of this written warning will be kept by the supervisor but it will be disregarded for disciplinary purposes after .... months subject to satisfactory conduct and performance.

Stage 3. Final written warning or disciplinary suspension. If there is still a failure to improve and conduct or performance is still unsatisfactory, or if the misconduct is sufficiently serious to warrant only one written warning but insufficiently serious to justify dismissal (in effect both first and final written warning), a **final written warning** will normally be given to the employee. This will give details of the complaint, will warn that dismissal will result if there is no satisfactory improvement and will advise of the right of appeal. A copy of this final written warning will be kept by the supervisor but it will be

Figure 9.2   ACAS model disciplinary procedure

spent after .... months (in exceptional cases the period may be longer) subject to satisfactory conduct and performance.

Alternatively, consideration will be given to imposing a penalty of a disciplinary suspension without pay for up to a maximum of five working days.

Stage 4. Dismissal. If conduct or performance is still unsatisfactory, and the employee still fails to reach the prescribed standards, **dismissal** will normally result. Only the appropriate Senior Manager can take the decision to dismiss. The employee will be provided, as soon as reasonably practicable, with written reasons for dismissal, the date on which employment will terminate and the right of appeal.

4 Gross misconduct

The following list provides examples of offences which are normally regarded as gross misconduct:

(a) Theft, fraud, deliberate falsification of records.
(b) Fighting, assault on another person.
(c) Deliberate damage to company property.
(d) Serious incapability through alcohol or being under the influence of illegal drugs.
(e) Serious negligence which causes unacceptable loss, damage or injury.
(f) Serious act of insubordination.

If you are accused of an act of gross misconduct, you may be suspended from work on full pay, normally for no more than five working days, while the company investigates the alleged offence. If, on completion of the investigation and the full disciplinary procedure, the company is satisfied that gross misconduct has occurred, the result will normally be summary dismissal without notice or payment in lieu of notice.

5 Appeals

An employee who wishes to appeal against a disciplinary decision should inform .... within two working days. The Senior Manager will hear all appeals and his/her decision is final. At the appeal any disciplinary penalty imposed will be reviewed but it cannot be increased.

Source: Advisory, Conciliation and Arbitration Service, *Discipline at Work: the ACAS advisory handbook*, 1990.

Figure 9.2   contd.

types of procedural arrangements. This, as recommended in the ACAS code, provides that for most types of disciplinary offence action will usually involve employees receiving an oral and two written warnings before they are dismissed. In doing so, both it and the ACAS code can be seen to be endorsing what has been labelled a corrective orientation to discipline, which emphasizes its role '. . . in deterring and educating workers rather than punishing them'.[27]

The adoption of a corrective orientation has been seen by some to reflect a more general move by employers over the post-war period away from the 'authoritarian' or 'coercive' approach to discipline that had previously predominated. This change, it is argued, was prompted by a number of operational considerations, including the adverse effects of the more punishment-oriented approach on worker morale and efficiency; the need to introduce greater consistency as work-force size increased; and the importance of retaining skilled labour in short supply.

Inevitably, a good deal of debate has taken place over how far such a shift of approach has, in practice, occurred among employers.[28] This debate usefully highlights the important point that decisions concerning how to handle disciplinary action cannot sensibly be divorced from considerations of how they relate to other aspects of human resource management and the operational environment of organizations more generally. Current developments in employer human-resource strategies serve to further illustrate this point.

In recent years, as noted in Chapter 2, many employers have, in response to the more hostile and competitive economic environment confronting them, embarked on radical reviews of their existing human-resource strategies in an attempt to improve labour recruitment, retention and utilization. These reviews have frequently resulted in important changes being made to payment and reward systems, 'production technologies' and supervisory practices and internal training and communication systems. Many of these changes have been aimed at securing greater commitment and flexibility from workers (see Chapter 5). That is, generating an environment in which workers can be trusted to carry out their responsibilities efficiently without the need for close monitoring and supervision.

At the same time, many employers have felt compelled to adopt a more rigorous approach to the enforcement of work rules and standards as they struggle to cope with less favourable financial and product market conditions. The net result of these two trends is that employers are frequently walking a delicate policy tightrope. On the other hand, competitive pressures are seen to require a tougher approach to discipline; on the other, these same pressures are prompting employers to adopt human-resource initiatives which are dependent for their success on the achievement of a greater degree of trust and co-operation between managers and those they manage. It takes no great insight to see that the first of these strategies can potentially undermine the second.

References

1. Kelly, J. and Nicholson, N., 'Strikes and other forms of industrial action', *Industrial Relations Journal*, **11**(5), 1980.
2. Fox, A., *Industrial Sociology and Industrial Relations*, Royal Commission Research Paper No. 3, London: HMSO, 1966.
3. Rhodes, S. R. and Steers, R. M., *Managing Employee Absenteeism*, Reading, MA: Addison-Wesley, 1990.
4. Edwards, P. K. and Scullion, H., *The Social Organisation of Industrial Conflict: Control and resistance in the workplace*, Oxford: Blackwell, 1982, chapter 4.
5. Walsh, K., 'Are disputes in decline? – evidence from UK industry', *Industrial Relations Journal*, **18**(1), 1987, pp. 7–13.
6. Salamon, M., *Industrial Relations: Theory and practice* (2nd edn), Englewood Cliffs, NJ: Prentice Hall, 1992.
7. *ibid.*
8. Hyman, R., *Strikes* (4th edn), London: Macmillan, 1990.
9. Millward, N., Stevens, M., Smart, D. and Hawes, W. R., *Workplace Industrial Relations in Transition: the DE/ESRC/PSI/ACAS surveys*, Aldershot: Gower, 1992.
10. Edwards, P. K., 'The patterns of collective industrial action', in *Industrial Relations in Britain*, ed. Bain, G., Oxford: Blackwell, 1983.
11. Edwards, P., 'Does PBR cause strikes?', *Industrial Relations Journal*, **18**(3), 1987, pp. 210–18.
12. See, for example, Morris, T. and Wood, S., 'Testing the survey method: continuity and change in British industrial relations', *Work, Employment and Society*, **5**, 1991, pp. 259–82.
13. Lord Wedderburn, 'Industrial relations and the courts', *Industrial Law Journal*, 1980, pp. 65–94.
14. Mackie, K., 'Changes in the law since 1979: an overview', in *A handbook of industrial relations practice* (3rd edn), ed. Towers, B., London: Kogan Page, 1992.
15. Trade Union and Labour Relations (Consolidation) Act, 1992, London: HMSO.
16. Lewis, in Towers, *A handbook of industrial relations practice*.
17. Turner, H. A., Roberts, G. and Roberts, D., *Management Characteristics and Labour Conflict*, Cambridge: Cambridge University Press, 1977.
18. Thomson, A. W. J. and Murray, V. V., *Grievance Procedures*, London: Saxon House, 1976.
19. Lewis, R., 'Strike-free deals and pendulum arbitration', *British Journal of Industrial Relations*, **28**, 1990.
20. *ibid.*; Wood, Sir John, 'Last offer arbitration', *British Journal of Industrial Relations*, **23**, 1985.
21. S.1 Employment Protection Act 1975.

22. Millward *et al.*, *Workplace Industrial Relations in Transition: the DE/ESRC/ PSI/ACAS surveys*.
23. Ashdown, R. T. and Baker, K. H., *In working order: a study of industrial discipline*, Department of Employment Manpower Papers No. 6, London: HMSO, 1973.
24. Employment Protection (Consolidation) Act 1978.
25. Advisory, Conciliation and Arbitration Service. Code of Practice on Disciplinary Rules and Procedures in Employment, 1977.
26. James, P. and Lewis, D., *Discipline*, London: Institute of Personnel Management, 1992.
27. Ashdown and Baker, *In Working Order: A study of industrial discipline*.
28. See, for example, Edwards, P. K. and Whitson, C., 'Industrial discipline: the control of attendance and the subordination of labour', *Work, Employment and Society*, 3(1), 1989, pp. 1–28.

10

Achieving an integrated approach

The various techniques and arrangements discussed in the preceding chapters have raised a host of policy issues relating to the management of people at work. The choices made in respect of these, as has been stressed throughout, have important implications for organizational performance via their mediating influence on such factors as labour turnover and absenteeism, work effort and productivity and management–worker relationships more generally.

It is not possible to put forward universal policy prescriptions as to the types of decisions that will have the most beneficial impact on organizational performance. What may suit one organization may not suit another, due to variations between them in matters such as the external labour and product market conditions confronting them, the types of goods and services they produce, the work processes carried out and the sorts of staff that are employed. What is clear, as a matter of logic, is that the decisions taken in respect of particular issues should, as far as possible, take due account of those reached regarding other aspects of the management of people and the short- and long-term business and financial needs of the organization concerned.

Unfortunately, there are good grounds for believing that British employers have all too frequently failed to do precisely this. Instead, in the words of two leading academics, many have continued to be pragmatic and opportunistic in how they approach personnel and industrial relations management.[1] In recent years, however, it has been argued that this situation shows signs of changing. The growing interest in and adoption of 'human-resource management' by organizations is frequently seen as an indication of this shift towards a more long-term and strategic orientation.

At a superficial level, it is undoubtedly true that the term human-resource management has now entered the common parlance of personnel and industrial relations academics and practitioners. Personnel departments have frequently been re-titled human-resource departments. The publication of textbooks on the subject has become something of a growth industry and many courses at both undergraduate and postgraduate levels now carry the title 'human-resource management'. However, it is still very much an open question how far this change of terminology signifies real changes in organizational practice, and hence whether human-resource management really constitutes a qualitatively different approach to previous traditions of people management.

Many attempts have been made to draw clear definitional and conceptual distinctions between human-resource management and the traditional practice of personnel and industrial-relations management. Some writers have argued that the former entails a shift towards a more 'humanistic' approach, which aims to place less emphasis on the imposition of external controls on workers and more on generating their commitment.[2] Others question whether this is so, and indeed suggest that many current initiatives are often concerned with securing greater control over workers while paying lip service to a softer, more humanistic way of treating them.[3]

Nevertheless, there does seem common agreement that, if human-resource management does represent a distinctive approach to personnel and industrial-relations management, the basis of this distinction is its emphasis on long-term, strategic planning which is clearly linked to more general business strategies. In other words, that moves towards it involve organizations in creating a greater degree of integration between the various people-management policies, and between those policies and the overall business strategy of organizations. A substantial degree of agreement also exists with regard to the types of policy initiatives that have accompanied the greater use of the term 'human-resource management'. Thus, these are typically noted to include: the establishment of greater links between the pay and performance of individual workers; the devolution of many aspects of people management to line managers; a commitment to staff-training and development; supervisory styles that place far more emphasis on empowering workers and exercising self-discipline; and attempts to improve communications with and the involvement of individual workers, while at the same time downgrading collectivist forms of representation (see Table 10.1).

The evidence presented in the earlier chapters suggests that many

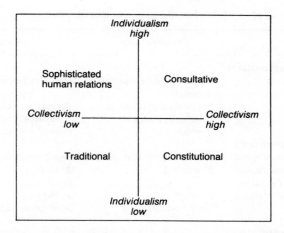

Source: Purcell, J., 'Mapping management style in employee relations', *Journal of Management Studies*, **24**, 1987, pp. 533–48.

Figure 10.1 Management style in handling employee relations

organizations over the past decade have indeed been adopting policies along these lines in order to develop the internal efficiency and flexibility they need to remain competitive. It does not, however, necessarily follow from this that their adoption can be taken as an indication that employers are in fact tending to adopt more long-term and strategic perspectives towards how they recruit, select, reward, utilize and deal with staff. Instead, it is perfectly possible that this coincidence of 'theory and practice' is yet another indication of the short-termism and fadishness that has historically marked employer actions in these areas.

However, if this apparent coming together of theory and practice does reflect the adoption of a new, more systematic approach to people issues, then it follows that employers are, albeit in very broad terms, engaged in a process of long-term convergence in how they deal with such issues. The practical implications of such a process of convergence can be illustrated by reference to Purcell's analysis of management 'styles'.

Purcell has argued that the approaches adopted by employers in the field of employee relations can be analyzed along two dimensions.[4] First, the degree of weight they attach to the welfare and development of individual employees and, secondly, the extent to which they provide for and embrace their collective representation. On the basis of this distinction between individualism and

Table 10.1   Twenty-seven points of difference

Dimension	Personnel and IR	HRM
Beliefs and assumptions		
1 Contract	Careful delination of written contracts	Aim to go 'beyond contract'
2 Rules	Importance of devising clear rules/mutuality	'Can-do' outlook; impatience with 'rule'
3 Guide to management action	Procedures	'Business-need'
4 Behaviour referent	Norms/custom and practice	Values/mission
5 Managerial task *vis-à-vis* labour	Monitoring	Nurturing
6 Nature of relations	Pluralist	Unitarist
7 Conflict	Institutionalized	De-emphasized
Strategic aspects		
8 Key relations	Labour-management	Customer
9 Initiatives	Piecemeal	Integrated
10 Corporate plan	Marginal to	Central to
11 Speed of decision	Slow	Fast
Line management		
12 Management role	Transactional	Transformational leadership
13 Key managers	Personnel/IR specialists	General/business/line managers
14 Communication	Indirect	Direct
15 Standardization	High (e.g. 'parity' an issue)	Low (e.g. 'parity' not seen as relevant)
16 Prized management skills	Negotiation	Facilitation
Key levers		
17 Selection	Separate, marginal task	Integrated, key task
18 Pay	Job evaluation (fixed grades)	Performance-related
19 Conditions	Separately negotiated	Harmonization
20 Labour-management	Collective bargaining contracts	Towards individual contracts
21 Thrust of relations with stewards	Regularized through facilities and training	Marginalized (with exception of some bargaining for change models)
22 Job categories and grades	Many	Few
23 Communication	Restricted flow	Increased flow
24 Job design	Division of labour	Teamwork
25 Conflict handling	Reach temporary truces	Manage climate and culture

Table 10.1 – contd.

Dimension	Personnel and IR	HRM
26 Training and development	Controlled access to courses	Learning companies
27 Foci of attention for interventions	Personnel procedures	Wide ranging cultural, structural and personnel strategies

IR, industrial relations; HRM, human-resource management.
Source: Storey, J., *Developments in the Management of Human Resources*, Oxford: Blackwell, 1992.

collectivism Purcell goes on to distinguish four distinct employee-relations management styles; traditional, sophisticated human relations, consultative and constitutional (see Figure 10.1).

Employers adopting a traditional style are seen to view labour as a factor of production and to assume that employee subordination is the 'natural order' of the employment relationship. For this reason trade-union organization is either resisted or kept at arm's length. Trade-union organization is similarly viewed with suspicion, if not outright opposition, by organizations practising sophisticated human relations. However, in this case employees are not treated as a mere factor of production, but considered to be the organization's most valuable resource. Such employers therefore often provide above-average pay and internal labour-market structures with clear promotion ladders. Considerable emphasis is also placed on good management–worker systems of communication, and reward structures that link individual pay and performance. In broad terms these characteristics are also apparent in what Purcell refers to as consultative organizations. A crucial difference between the two, however, is that the latter not only recognize unions but seek to incorporate them into the organization through the widespread disclosure of information and the establishment of extensive systems of consultation. The final style, that of the constitutionalist, also recognizes unions, but seeks to limit union involvement to issues unconnected to operational and strategic management issues. More generally, these organizations tend, at least for unskilled and semi-skilled workers, to adopt a similar value structure as the traditionalists with regard to the treatment of staff.

In discussing these different styles, Purcell stresses that they are of little relevance to the vast majority of British organizations, for the simple reason that they do not have a clear style of employee-relations management. The current interest in human-resource management, however, would suggest that this situation is changing. Moreover, the types of practices typically associated with the concept further suggest that a growing number of organizations are aspiring towards the style of management labelled 'sophisticated human relations'.

Available evidence, as noted above, lends some weight to this last observation. However, it also suggests that many organizations with aspirations of this type are still a long way from achieving such a style of management. For example, a large survey of 137 multi-establishment enterprises found that while over 80 per cent of firms claimed to have an overall policy or philosophy for the management of employees, only half said this was in a written document and less than a quarter reported that a copy of such a document was given to employees.[5]

Furthermore, there is growing evidence that many organizations are struggling to maintain the changed programmes they have introduced, due to a lack of resources and stability.[6] As a result, all too often the process of long-term change is being undermined by short-term financial and business pressures, which necessitate actions that sit uncomfortably with, if not undermine, the ethos on which the overall reform process is based. For example, appraisal systems are introduced without the support of the mechanisms needed to meet the training and development needs identified through them; initiatives to empower workers are accompanied by the simultaneous tightening of disciplinary practices; and statements about organizational commitment to employment security and staff development are made against the background of large-scale redundancies.

These types of tension can be viewed as at least partly inevitable, given the difficult financial and trading conditions that have frequently confronted employers in recent years. However, it has been argued convincingly that this problem of maintaining the change process is also a reflection of more fundamental features of the British economy, which mitigate against the establishment of long-term human-resource strategies. These features are seen to include: the underprovision of management education and training; devolved systems of management control which place priority on meeting immediate performance targets; the dominance of the finance function in British companies; and the extent to which private-sector organizations are owned by institutional investors with short-run investment horizons.[7]

Therefore it would seem that the evolution of a long-term strategic approach to the management of people still has a long way to go in much of British industry: despite the fact that there is growing evidence to support the view that the lack of such an approach damages the international competitiveness of many parts of British industry. More generally, the main lesson that would seem to emerge from recent developments is that the strategic integration of personnel and industrial-relations policies, both with each other and with overall business strategies, is critically dependent on the presence of an economic and organizational environment that is supportive of long-term investment and planning. The achievement of such an environment is arguably one of the greatest challenges facing British organizations today.

References

1. Purcell, J. and Sisson, K., 'Strategies and practice in the management of industrial relations', in *Industrial Relations in Britain*, ed. Bain, G. S., Oxford: Blackwell, 1983.
2. See, for example, Walton, R., 'From control to commitment in the workplace'. *Harvard Business Review*, **63**, March–April 1985.
3. Storey, J., *Developments in the Management of Human Resources*, Oxford: Blackwell, 1992.
4. Purcell, J., 'Mapping management style in employee relations', *Journal of Management Studies*, **24**, 1987, pp. 533–48. For a critique of this model see Marchington, M. and Parker, P., *Changing Patterns of Employee Relations*, Hemel Hempstead: Harvester Wheatsheaf, 1990.
5. Marginson, P., Edwards, P. K., Martin, R., Purcell, J. and Sisson, K., *Beyond the Workplace: Managing industrial relations in multi-establishment enterprises*, Oxford: Blackwell, 1988.
6. See, for example, Snape, E., Redman, T. and Wilkinson, A., 'Human resource management in building societies: making the transformation?', *Human Resource Management Journal*, **3**(3), 1993, pp. 43–60.
7. Storey, J. and Sisson, K., 'Limits to transformation: human resource management in the British context', *Industrial Relations Journal*, **21**, 1990, pp. 60–5.

Index